Develop Your

Business Plan

by Richard L. Leza

and

Jose F. Placencia

_____

Published by The Oasis Press

Milpitas, California

Published by Oasis Press*
720 S. Hillview Drive
Milpitas, CA 95035
408/263-9671

International Standard Book Number 0-916378-21-7

Library of Congress Catalog Number 82-081323

Printed in the United States of America

10 9 8 7

*Division of Publishing Services, Inc., a Texas Corporation

CONTENTS

MARKET ANALYSIS

STRATEGIC PLANNING

MANAGEMENT TEAM

FINANCIAL ANALYSIS

FOREWORD

Why plan? Why develop a **business** plan?

If you have ever been unhappy with the past performance of your business, or if you believe that your business could grow faster, make more profit, or be more competitive, you have reason to plan. You cannot do anything about the past, and you have very little impact on the present. But you can control the future.

The authors have helped hundreds of small and medium-sized businesses in California's Silicon Valley to develop their business plans. The positive results have taught the entrepreneur to appreciate the role that planning plays in a successful venture.

This book will help you to produce a step-by-step guide to the planning process. It will help you to produce a formal business plan; one that is well thought-out and professionally presented. This guide was developed to achieve that end.

Whatever your business, a well thought-out plan will put you ahead of the competition and will interest others in your venture. Time spent in planning now will save time and dollars later.

Richard L. Leza
Jose F. Placencia

Santa Clara, California
January, 1985

INTRODUCTION

Planning is the systematic development of actions aimed at reaching business objectives. It involves analyzing, evaluating, and selecting opportunities. A business plan is a detailed written statement that tells why, how, and when a company will achieve specific objectives.

After preparing the plan, management should adopt a business strategy for action. Key personnel, prospective investors, and other interested parties should know precisely how management will use the money and resources at its disposal. Management's primary responsibility is to secure the business's future. This should be accomplished through orderly planning. It should not be left to chance.

If you are starting a business, a business plan will help you to define your concept, evaluate the competition, determine your risks, and estimate your costs. A shortened version of a business plan, sometimes called a *private offering*, is often prepared to summarize the business for initial investors. Prospective investors from whom commitments can be developed should be given a copy of the complete business plan.

The length and sequence of a business plan will vary with the complexity of the business. But every plan contains the six essential elements. These are: where, why, how, when, who, and what. **Where** the business is to be located may be determined by considering its purpose, the competition, the capabilities of management and the opportunities for success. **Why** the business will succeed is determined by identifying market and product advantages. **How** describes the company's resources and it's ability to carry out the plan. **When** the business arrives, is indicated by milestones measured in profits, sales calls, number of employees, and so forth, as per the plan. **Who** defines each person's specific responsibilities for accomplishing the goals of the business. **What** it costs is indicated by the cash flow projections.

The purpose of *Develop Your Business Plan* is to provide you with a step-by-step guide to this process. The guide is designed to help you:

1. Analyze your existing business or determine the feasibility and desirability of starting a new one

2. Plan for the your company's future

3. Raise capital from outside sources

4. Develop a detailed marketing and operational plan

As you analyze your industry, your market, and your own company, you will become aware of many important issues, which you can then put into a clearer perspective. You will also begin to understand where your company has come from and where you would like it to go. You will have a business plan to guide the growth of your firm. And you will have a document that you can submit to banks, investors, and management consultants.

The business and new venture planning process is shown in graphic form on the following pages. They consist of six steps; the steps that are shaded are the most important ones and should receive the most attention. To complete the plan, you need not know anything about planning methods or strategies. But you must know your business and understand the key factors that influence it.

Business Planning Process

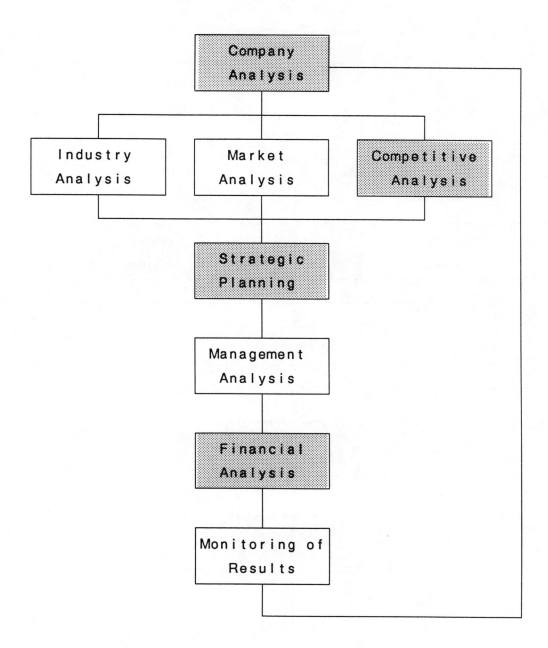

New Venture Planning Process

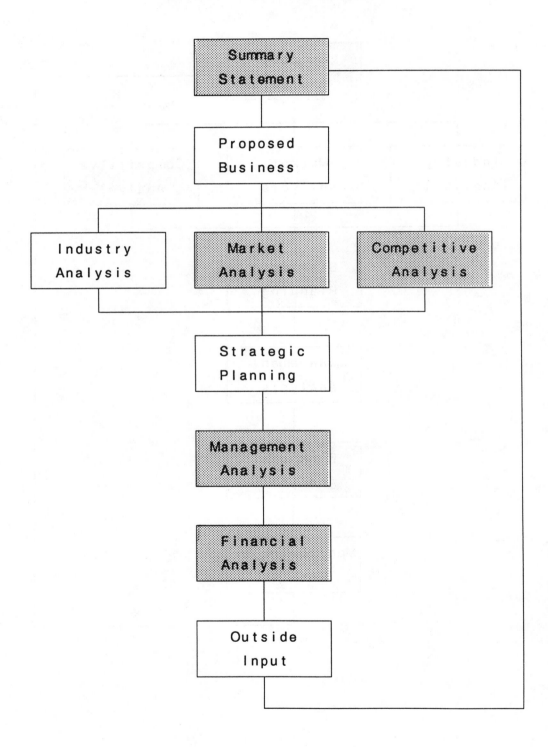

SUMMARY STATEMENT

The Summary Statement is used to summarize and emphasize the high points of the business plan. It should enable prospective investors or managers within the company to identify and understand the company's objectives and strengths. Although the Summary Statement appears first in the business plan, it should not be written until the plan has been completed. The extracts from the plan should be presented as indicated below. They should be no longer than a few pages.

Summary Statement

Present Status of Company

Present the current company statistical status in a short paragraph. Include information about profitability, sales, products or services, employees, and other major company indicators.

Present Status

Strategic Opportunities

The *strategic opportunities* are the overall objective of the business plan. Discuss how company objectives and strategies will be developed to achieve projected profits.

Strategic Opportunities

Company Thrust

Company thrust is a statement of an industry overview. Discuss the competition, the risk, and the company's capabilities and objectives.

Company thrust

Business Strategies

The choice of *business strategies* should be based on needs, objectives, and company thrust selected. From the company thrust selected, the appropriate business stategies should be identified. However, not more than three strategies should be implemented during an established time schedule. Remember that you need not attempt to pursue all the strategies associated with a company thrust.

Business Strategies

Resource Requirements

State the resources needed to meet the objectives stated in the plan, such as money, people, management, and so forth.

```
Resource Requirements
```

Expected Benefits

Describe how the company and the investor will benefit when the
company achieves its objectives. How much equity, if applicable, are
you willing to sell?

Expected Benefits

Net Cash Requirements

The analysis of *net cash requirements* should be based on assump-ons of the business plan (total costs, revenues, strategies selected, projected sales, net cash flow, and so forth) of all products or services lines. All major categories should be listed as line items and totaled to calculate the cash required to operate the business.

Net Cash Requirements				
	Year			
	19__	19__	19__	19__
Total receipts				
Disbursements				
Cost of Sales				
Total expenses				
(minus depreciation				
Capital expenditures				
Other				
Total disbursements				
Total cashflow				

EXAMPLE	Net Cash Requirements			
	Year			
	1986	1987	1988	1989
Total receipts ($000)	2,400	7,000	15,500	28,000
Disbursements				
Cost of Sales	1,865	5,600	9,350	15,650
Total expenses	1,190	3,100	5,200	7,000
(minus depreciation				
Capital expenditures	500	500	1,000	1,000
Other	100	100	0	0
Total disbursements	3,655	9,300	15,500	23,650
Total cashflow($000)	(1,225)	(2,300)	0	4,350

Performance Measures and Milestones

Performance measures and milestones should include both financial and nonfinancial indicators of the company's success in implementing its strategy. Financial indicators may include sales, unit costs and prices, average order size, and level of debt. Nonfinancial indicators may include number of customers, inventory turnover, order backlogs, products developed, and number of employees.

Performance Measures and Milestones

COMPANY ANALYSIS

Historical Data

What business are you in or do you intend to enter?

This section should contain a brief but comprehensive history of your company. It should highlight the key influences that have affected the business since it was formed. For example:

o The history of your company

o The purpose of the company now or when it was formed

o The role each principal played in the company's development

o Events that affected the product's development

o Current organizational structure and key personnel

o Historical and current trends in sales and financial performance (*FINANCIAL PERFORMANCE INDICATOR CHART, ACTUAL MONTHLY SALES*, and *ACTUAL YEAR-TO-DATE SALES*. Samples of actual monthly and year-to-year sales are also included.)

```
┌────────────────────────────────────────────────────────────┐
│  Historical Data (What business are you in or do you        │
│     intend to enter?)                                        │
│                                                              │
│                                                              │
│                                                              │
│                                                              │
│                                                              │
│                                                              │
│                                                              │
│                                                              │
│                                                              │
└────────────────────────────────────────────────────────────┘
```

Background: Financial Performance Indicator (History)[*]				
EXAMPLE	Year			
Key Indicators	19<u>82</u>	19<u>83</u>	19<u>84</u>	19<u>85</u>
Income data				
Net sales ($000)	N/A	N/A	250	1,000
Cost of goods sold			200	700
Gross profit			50	300
Operating expenses			(200)	(700)
Net profit after taxes			(150)	(400)
Asset/liability data				
Accounts receivable			60	200
Inventory			32	180
Total assets			190	500
Accounts payable			40	150
Short term debt			0	0
Long term debt			40	150
total Liabilities			100	300
Net Worth			90	200
Ratios (see *Industry Analysis*)				
Current			0.72	1.21
Total debt to total assests			.53	0.60
Collection period			45 days	60 days
Net sales to inventory			7.81	5.55
Net profit margin after taxes			(60%)	(40%)
Return on net worth			-	-

*These are historical data on key indicators which are partial representations and not a true picture of the Income Statement or Balance Sheet of company.

Background: Financial Performance Indicator (History)				
	Year			
Key Indicators	19__	19__	19__	19__
Income data				
Net sales				
Cost of goods sold				
Gross profit				
Operating expenses				
Net profit after taxes				
Asset/liability data				
Accounts receivable				
Inventory				
Total assets				
Accounts payable				
Short term debt				
Long term debt				
total Liabilities				
Net Worth				
Ratios (see *Industry Analysis)*				
Current				
Total debt to total assests				
Collection period				
Net sales to inventory				
Net profit margin after taxes				
Return on net worth				

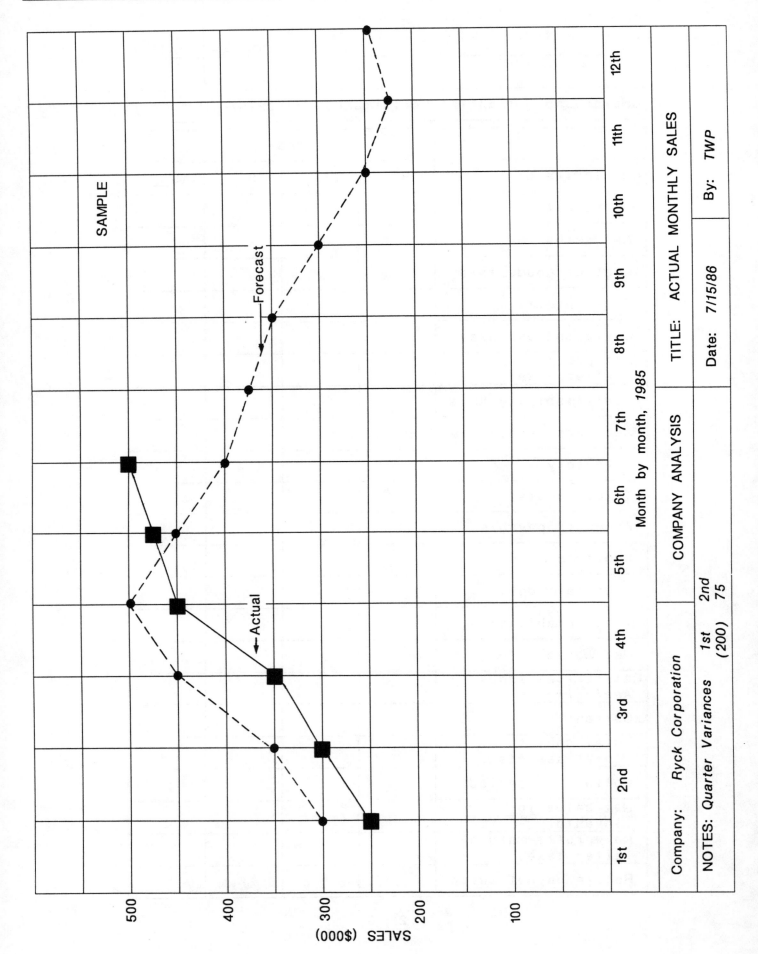

													1st		
													2nd		
													3rd		
													4th		
													5th	COMPANY ANALYSIS	
													6th		
													7th		
													8th	TITLE:	
													9th		
													10th		By:
													11th	Date:	
													12th		

Company:

NOTES:

SALES ($000)

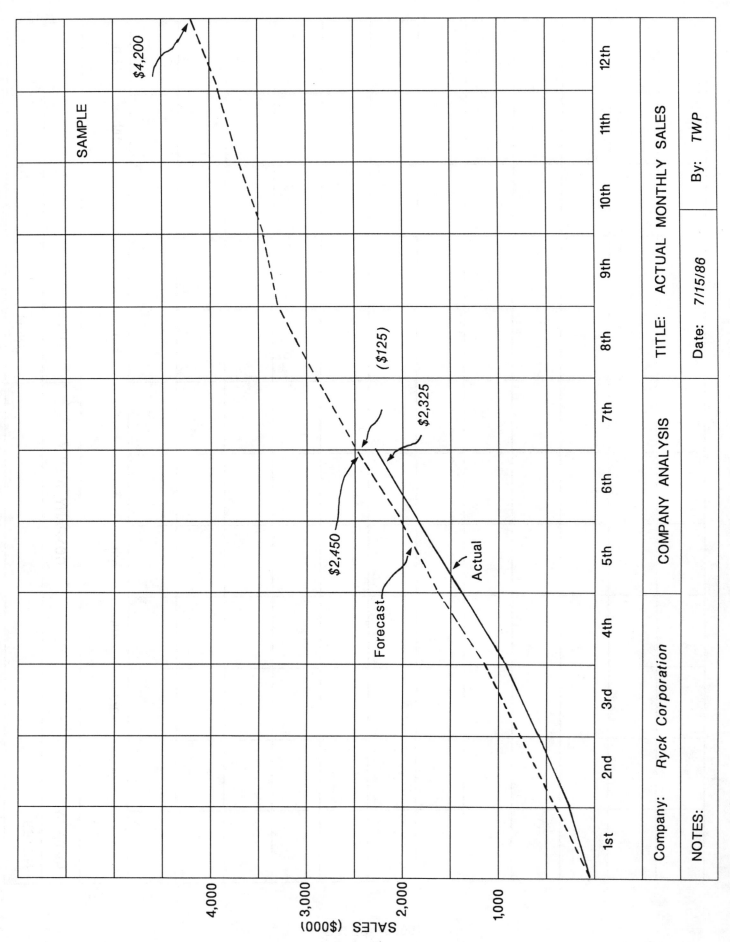

1st	2nd	3rd	4th	5th	6th	7th	8th	9th	10th	11th	12th		

Company:

COMPANY ANALYSIS

TITLE:

Date:

By:

NOTES:

SALES ($000)

Products

What products or services are you in or do you intend to develop?

Note whether you are offering goods or services. Describe how your product or service lines differ from those of your competitors. (A **product or service line** is a *family* of related products or services.) Include product brochures in the Appendix of your business plan.

Products (What products or services are you in or do you intend to develop?)

Markets

What markets are you in or do you intend to penetrate?

List the major market segments served by your company. (A **market segment** is a group of customers who exhibit some common customer need, buying habit, or other characteristic.) Specify the size of the market and the size of your company's share of the market.

Markets (What markets are you in or do you intend to penetrate?)

Customers

Who and where are the major purchasers?

Indicate whether the company's business is conducted with many or only a few customers. List the company's primary customers.

Customers (Who and where are the major purchasers?)

What is the status of your current technology?

Compare the technology of your company with that of your competitors or anticipated competitors. State why you think it is superior, compar- able, or inferior. In which areas of technology is the company particularly strong? If there are impor- tant weaknesses in technology, indicate what they are and how they can be overcome.

Technology Position (What is the status of your current technology?)

Forward or Backward Integration

Is integration important to your company?

Describe the degree to which your company is forward or backward integrated. (A **backward integrated** company owns or controls its supply systems. A **forward integrated** company owns or controls its distribution systems.)

Forward or Backward Integration? (Is integration important to your company?)

Cost Comparisons

What are your costs?

Compare your company's costs with the industry composite. To find the industry composite, start by checking with industry associations. Many of them publish average cost information and financial ratios by Standard Industrial Classification code numbers. (For example, **Robert Morris Associates Annual Statement Studies**). If cost data are not available, the best approach is to list the principal cost components (for example, capital, labor, materials, and overhead) of your company. Estimate your competitors' costs and compare them with your costs.

Cost Comparistons (What are your costs?)

Operational Resources

What is required to conduct your company's business?

Describe the facilities, space, capital equipment, master schedule, and labor force required to conduct your company's business. For a manufacturing business, describe scheduling, purchasing, inventory, and production control. For a service business, describe location, equipment leasing, space, and labor force.

Complete the chart entitled *OPERATIONAL FACILITIES* for each location used or requested by the company. For an existing business, describe the facilities that are currently being used. Analyze each facility according to its function (office, storage, factory) and assign the appropriate building work space.

For a new business, describe how and when the necessary facilities will be acquired. Will equipment and space be leased or purchased? How much of the proposed financing will be devoted to facility and equipment?

For each facility include the following information:

Location. Be specific. If your company rents in a large building, specify the floor or suite number as well as the address.

Use and size. Indicate whether the space is used for offices, for storage, for a factory, and so on.

Capacity. Estimate the capacity of each facility (and its associated equipment) in terms of output per hour, units per day, number of workers that can be accommodated, or whatever other unit of measurement is appropriate for your company. The estimate should be in terms of your preferred capacity, which may not be the same as the rated capacity for a particular facility.

Capacity utilization. Estimate the percentage of the capacity of each facility that is currently being used. For example, the warehouse is usually 80 percent full.

Equipment. List the types and amount of major equipment in each facility. Include manufacturing equipment, vehicles, office machines, furniture, and fixtures.

Age/Capacity. Discuss the physical condition and age of the existing equipment. Include the number of units that can be produced, what equipment is old or obsolete and must be replaced, and so on.

Equipment Utilization. Estimate the percentage of utilization for each piece of equipment currently being used.

Operational Resources (What is required to conduct
the company's business?)

OPERATION FACILITIES

Facility Location	Use	Size (sq ft)	Capacity	Utilization (%)	Equipment	Age/ Capacity	Utilization (%)
Santa Clara, CA	Admin. Marketing	3,500	25 employees	90%	3 IBM PCs 1 DEC computer	2 years/ 3 persons	70%
San Jose, CA	Manufacturing	7,000	50 units per day	50%	Computer tester Solder machines	1 year 50 units/ day	50%

OPERATION FACILITIES

Facility Location	Use	Size (sq ft)	Capacity	Utilization (%)	Equipment	Age/ Capacity	Utilization (%)

Company Strengths and Weakesses

What major strengths or weaknesses can be identified?

Use the chart entitled *COMPANY STRENGTHS AND WEAKNESSES* to describe the principal operating functions of your company and the resources used to perform them. Determine your position in relation to the competition. Some cells will not be relevant to your company, leave them blank. On the right-hand side of the chart, summarize your company's major strengths and weaknesses in resources.

Functions are defined as follows:

Marketing. The activities involved in administration and sales. Marketing may include sending salespeople into the field.

Finance. The activities involved in collecting and disbursing money, including bookkeeping and other financial record keeping, budgeting, credit and collections, accounts payable, long-term financial planning, and raising capital for the business.

Purchasing. The purchase of necessary equipment, materials, and supplies needed on an ongoing or periodic basis. Purchasing also includes maintaining appropriate inventories of materials and supplies.

Distribution. The series of steps by which a product or service is delivered to the customer.

Resources are defined as follows:

Information systems. Adequate automated data-processing support for each functional area.

Policies and procedures. Effective guidelines and mechanisms for planning, implementing, and controlling activities in each functional area.

Management. Effective management skills and efficient reporting systems that provide information used for decision making.

EXAMPLE

Company Strengths and Weaknesses

Functions	Strong (+)	Aver- age (0)	Weak (-)	Major Strengths and/or Weaknesses in Resources
General administration		0		
Marketing	+			*Experience - V.P. of marketing*
Finance			-	*Need full time controller*
Human resources		0		
Engineering	+			*three key engineers*
Operations		0		*need material planners and quality engineers*
Production	+			
Purchasing	+			
Distribution			-	*Need to establish distribution channels*
International				*N/A - domestic concentration*
Servicing Dept.	+			

Functions	Strong (+)	Aver-age (0)	Weak (-)	Major Strengths and/or Weaknesses in Resources
General administration				
Marketing				
Finance				
Human resources				
Engineering				
Operations				
Production				
Purchasing				
Distribution				
International				

Company Strengths and Weaknesses

Bases of Competition

Why do customers buy from your company or from your competitors?

Bases of competition are known characteristics that customers use to choose among competitors. They include price, technology, service, quality, reputation, location, and delivery time, among other things. Almost every industry has nearly all of these characteristics. The bases of competition are the particular characteristics that most buyers use to make their selection.

For example, ABC company manufactures micro- computers. It buys its electronic keyboard's from the supplier who offers the best quality and the best delivery time. ABC also considers technology in choosing a supplier, because the supplier will be responsible for designing the circuit logic. Price is not a basis of competition, because the electronic keyboard represents only a small percentage of the total product cost.

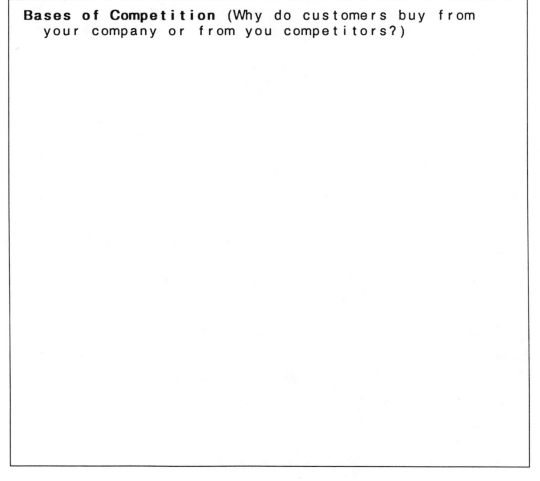

Bases of Competition (Why do customers buy from your company or from you competitors?)

Key Success Factors

What are your company's key success factors?

A company's **key success factors** are the ways in which it achieves its competition. For example, if price is an important basis of competition being the low-cost producer is the corresponding key success factor. Depending on the structure of the industry, the key success factor might be refined to having low variable costs. When reputation is a basis of competition, the corresponding key success factor may be good quality control and field service. For each basis of competition that you identified, list one or more key success factors by which you can achieve it.

Key Success Factors (What are your company's key success factors?)

Competitive Position

Who are your major competitors?

The next step is to analyze your company's relative competitive position. To do this, you will use the COMPETITIVE POSITION chart.

Begin by listing the bases of competition and key success factors you identified in the previous sections (items a and b). List them in descending order of importance.

Next use a weighting system to rate the bases of competition and key success factors (item c). For example, the two most important bases of competition might be weighted 5 and 4, with the rest weighted 3, 2, or 1. Do not weight all the bases of competition equally. The purpose of weighting is to show that a company can be a successful competitor if it does well with the industry's key success factors.

Now list your major industry competitors (item d), beginning with your company.

Next score each competitor relative to the others on each of the bases of competition and key success factors. The scoring system (item e) is applied as follows:

+1   strong competitor
 0   average competitor
- 1   weak competitor

For example, in an industry where price is very important, the average price of a particular product is $20, and most competitors' prices range between $18 and $23. The single competitor whose price is $18 would be scored +1, while the others would be scored 0. A competitor who entered the market with a comparable item priced at $25 would be scored -1.

When you have scored each competitor on each of the bases of competition and key success factors, the next step is to compute total scores. Multiply the score for each competitor by the weight previously assigned. Then sum up the figures under item h, adding positive scores and subtracting negative scores to arrive at weighted totals (items f and g). Using the weighted totals, rank all the strong competitors and all the weak competitors (item h). All other competitors not ranked in these two categories are assumed to be average competitors.

Competitive Position			EXAMPLE							
(a) Bases of Competition	(c) Weight	Self		(d) Major Competitors						
				ABC		RST		XYZ		
		e	h	e	h	e	h	e	h	e	h
Price	5	0	0	1	5	0	0	-1	-5		
Quality	4	1	4	0	0	0	0	0	0		
Volume	3	0	0	1	3	1	3	0	0		
Technology	1	1	1	1	1	0	0	1	1		
(f) Weighted totals			5		9		3		-4		
(b) Key success factors											
Low cost of manufacture	5	0	0	1	5	0	0	-1	-5		
Quality control	4	1	4	0	0	0	0	0	0		
Delivery time	3	0	0	1	3	1	3	0	0		
Reliability	1	1	1	1	1	0	0	0	0		
(g) Weighted totals			5		9		3		-5		
(h) Final rankings			10		18		6		-9		

Strong	Weak
ABC	XYZ

Competitive Position												
(a) Bases of Competition	(c) Weight	Self		(d) Major Competitors								
		e	h	e	h	e	h	e	h	e	h	e	h
(f) Weighted totals												
(b) Key success factors												
(g) Weighted totals												
(h) Final rankings												
Strong					Weak							

INDUSTRY ANALYSIS

Definition

Analyze the current status of the industry and forecast the conditions in which your business now operates or will operate in the future. Describe the principal companies with which you compete directly or indirectly. (Companies that offer the same product or the same service in the same market are competing directly. Companies that offer similar or substitute products in the same or an overlapping market are competing indirectly.) The industry definition should include:

o A description of the *economic sector* that the industry occupies—manufacturing, distribution (wholesale or retail), or services.

o A list of the *range of products* or *services* offered by the industry.

o A description of the *geographic scope* of the industry—whether local, regional, national, or international. (This is the geographic scope of the overall industry. It is determined by the markets in which products or services are offered by most competitors, not by the size or scope of individual companies.)

The industry definition may also include a listing of major products or market segments. For example, a computer manufacturer could divide its industry into five market segments: personal computers, microcomputers, minicomputers, main frames, and business that does not involve computers. Few competitors operate in this many segments; most operate in one or two.

It is not really difficult to define your industry. The idea is to find a definition that is broad enough to include all of your company's major competitors but specific enough to permit useful comparisons. However, a definition that is too broad is better than one that is too narrow.

```
Industry  Definitiion
```

Industry Size and Growth Rate

Determine the current size of the industry for your product or service. To determine size of the industry, refer to published data and talk to experts. Then estimate the total industry size in annual dollars or units. From this determine the industry annual growth rate and compare it to your projected annual growth rate. You will gain valuable information by estimating your competitors' growth rate relative to your own growth.

Growth rate may also be stated in terms of percentage increase or decrease in growth. If sales data are not available or are inapplicable, unit volume production or employment may be used. Explain your company's position in relation to the industry as a whole. At what rate is your business growing as compared to the industry?

Sources for industry information include the United States Government, industry associations, and general business publications, which are available at most large public libraries. Suggested resources include:

o US Government **Annual Survey of Manufacturers**. This publication provides data for the United States and individual states at the four-digit Standard Industrial Classification (SIC) code level.

o **Construction Review**. This publication reports on the value of residential construction by state, and on the value of nonresidential construction by region.

o State resale sales tax offices. Most states report information on taxable retail sales by type of outlet and geographic area.

Industry Publications. Most industry publications are listed in the **Business Periodicals Index**, which is available in most public libraries. Typical titles are **Chemical Marketing Reporter**, **Electronic News**, **Food Service Marketing**, and **Merchandising**.

General business publications. These periodical include **Forbes**, **Fortune**, and **Business Week**, the last of which publishes sales figures for industry groups on a quarterly basis.

Although there is plenty of information available, most small companies will find it difficult to use. Most data available will frequently not correspond to industry definition and geographic scope as selected by your company. Therefore, industry size and growth must be estimated. You can also estimate industry size by estimating the sizes of your competitors and totaling these estimates. Using this total, you can then estimate total industry sales by dividing by competitors estimated market share.

Industry Size and Growth Rate

Key Growth Factors

Key growth factors are trends and conditions beyond the control of
the industry or of the companies within the industry. There are
significant growth factors that affect the industry's market size and
level of demand. There are also *strong forces* that drive primary
demand. For example, the key growth factors that influence a small
manufacturer of electronic parts for automobiles include automobile
production in the United States, economic trends in the United States,
and trade relations between the United States and foreign manufacturers. The effects of these events on a small company may not be
apparent, but they are quite real nonetheless.

The distinction between primary and secondary growth factors is
somewhat arbitrary. The best approach is to list **all** the growth
factors that seem reasonable to you and then describe how they
affect your company. It is important to identify negative as well as
positive growth factors. If you list a great many growth factors,
highlight the most important ones.

Key Growth Factors

Cyclicality

Cyclical industries are those whose long term performance rises and falls as a result of external economic cycles, usually the national business cycle. Cyclical industries generally do well during periods of strong growth and do poorly during recessions. Typical cyclical industries are automobile manufacturing, residential construction, air travel, and machine tool manufacturing.

There are a few countercyclical industries. These industries do relatively better in recessions than in good times. Portions of the construction industry exhibit this pattern, because the government may fund public works projects during recessions to offset unemployment.

Cyclical patterns for local or regional industries should be identified and specific strengths or weaknesses associated with the locality should be stated.

Cyclicality

Seasonality

Seasonality refers to the distribution of business activity throughout the year. Identify your industry seasonal pattern and estimate the sales distribution throughout the year. If an industry lacks a seasonal pattern, it is reasonable to expect that its sales will be distributed fairly evenly throughout the year. Seasonal industries have a disproportionate amount of activity in one part of the year and correspondingly less in the others. For example, ski retailers do about 60 percent of their year's business in the four winter months. Construction is typically a seasonal industry, although this is truer in some parts of the country than in others.

Seasonality

Industry Life Cycle

When you assess *industry life cycle*, remember that you are considering the industry as a whole. Industry maturity is divided into four broad stages: Embryonic, Growth, Mature, and Aging. These stages reflect the life cycle of an industry. The chart entitled *INDUSTRY LIFE CYCLE* shows the sales history of a typical industry following the four broad stages.

To determine your industry's current stage of maturity, review the criteria listed in the left hand column of the chart. For each criterion, indicate the current stage of maturity of your industry by putting an X in the appropriate column. If the stage of maturity is changing in some cases, put in two Xs to indicate the direction of change.

Once you have filled out the chart, you can determine overall industry stage of maturity by looking at the distribution of Xs. If most of the criteria fall into the Mature segment of this matrix, the industry life cycle is currently at the stage of Mature. If a few fall into the Embryonic matrix and a few into the Mature matrix, the stage is in Late Growth moving into Mature. There are no absolute rules as to when an industry moves from one stage of maturity to another.

An industry in the Embryonic stage, like electronic measuring instrumentation, is characterized by rapid growth and volatile market shares. An industry in the Growth stage, like microcomputers, is characterized by rapid growth (where market share and technology have been established). In addition, the barriers to entry are beginning to be defined. An industry in the Mature stage, like steel, is characterized by a stable market size, stable share of the market, and a stable technology. Finally, an industry in the Aging stage, like black-and-white television, is best characterized by narrow profit margins, falling demand, and declining competition.

Industry Life Cycle			*Example*	
Criteria	Embry-onic	Growth	Mature	Aging
Growth rate	*high*	*high*	*stable*	*low*
Market share	*low*	*high*	*high*	*low*
Product line	*narrow*	*prolif-eration*	*no change*	*shrink-ing*
Financial	*cash hungry*	*med. earnings med.debt*	*cash rich low debt*	*cash low low earn low debt*
Number of competitors	*few*	*increase rapidly*	*stable and shakeout*	*declines*
Market share stability	*volatile*	*solid*	*en-trenched*	*concen-trated*
Purchasing patterns	*weak loyalty*	*moderate loyalty*	*strong loyalty*	*strong loyalty*
Ease of entry	*easy*	*usually easy*	*diffi-cult*	*No incen-tive*
Technology	*impor-tant break-through*	*Pefor-mance very im-portant*	*Refined seek ef-ficiency*	*Nominal role*
Typical volume growth rate		*time*		
Managerial style	*entre-preneur*	*sophis-ticated manager*	*critical admin-istrator*	*oppor-tunistic*
Overall stage				

Industry Life Cycle				
Criteria	Embry-onic	Growth	Mature	Aging
Growth rate				
Market share				
Product line				
Financial				
Number of competitors				
Market share stability				
Purchasing patterns				
Ease of entry				
Technology				
Typical volume growth rate				
Managerial style				
Overall stage				

Financial Operating Characteristics and Trends

You will need to compare **financial operating characteristics** that are directly related to your business with corresponding characteristics that are related to the overall industry. This may be difficult. There will be differences with respect to definitions, product lines, small sample set, statistical reliability, and so forth. The best approach is to use some or all of the sources listed below, noting any possible problems or inconsistencies. Financial data obtained from these sources should be used only as a general guideline.

o **Government documents.** The Bureau of the Census publishes the **Annual Survey of Manufacturers** as well as censuses of retail trade, wholesale trade, and transporations. The census publications include information about sales, inventories, and capital investments for many types of businesses. Annual publications provide less detailed updates of basic information.

o **General business publications. Forbes, Fortune,** and **Business Week** all publish information about financial performance and industry groups. **Forbes,** for example, publishes an annual issue reporting on profitability and growth trends of American industries. This includes industry median figures for net profit margins, return on equity and total capital, and debt/equity ratios. Probably the most widely known and used industry ratios are those compiled by Dun and Bradstreet. D & B provides fourteen ratios calculated for a large number of industries. These ratios are identified by an asterisk in the following pages. The annual statement studies compiled and published by Robert Morris Associates are based on financial statements received by banks in connection with loans.

o **Other sources.** Perhaps the best sources of industry financial infortion are industry associations and trade publications. **Ayer's Directory of Publications** lists trade publications by industry and geographic area.

Use basic financial ratios to evaluate your company's past and present position. These ratios will enable you to estimate your chances of acquiring funds. For example, a bank that is considering granting long-term leverage will emphasize earning power and operating efficiency. The firm must be able to repay its debts as well as earn profits.

Ratios are classified into four basic types: liquidity, leverage, activity, and profitability. Calculate two of each type. Select the ratios that are most important to your company. Remember that a ratio is not very meaningful in itself. To be useful, ratios must be compared in a trend analysis and to competitors' or the industry. Use the chart titled *FINANCIAL OPERATING CHARACTERISTICS* to compare your company's performance to that of the industry.

From financial indicators for each item listed, estimate an appropriate percentage or ratio (range) and indicate any obvious trends. (See the following pages for definitions.)

Financial Operating Characteristics					
	Industry *			Company		
	1984	1985	1986	1984	1985	1986
Assets	Not avail.		Not avail.			
Accts & notes receiv.		1,500		60	200	
Inventory ($000)		5,000		32	180	
Total current		6,500		92	380	
Fixed current (net)		4,000		98	120	
TOTAL ASSETS		10,500		190	500	
Liabilities						
Accts & note payable		2,000		50	150	
Total current		3,000		50	150	
Long-term debt		3,000		40	150	
Net worth		4,500		90	200	
TOTAL LIAB.& NET WORTH		10,500		190	500	
Income						
Net sales ($000)		22,000		250	1,000	
Cost of goods sold		13,200		200	700	
Gross profit		8,800		50	300	
Operating expenses		6,000		200	700	
Operating profit		2,800		(150)	(400)	
Other expenses (net)		160		-	-	
PROFIT BEFORE TAXES		2,640		(150)	(400)	
Ratios						
Current		2.16		1.84	2.53	
Total debt/total asset		0.57		0.53	0.60	
T debt/tang. net worth		1.3		1.0	1.5	
Collection period days		60		45	60	
Net sales/inventory		4.4		7.81	5.55	
Total assets turnover		2.09		1.32	2.0	
Gross profit margin		40%		20%	30%	
Operating profit marg.		-		-	-	
Return on net worth		27%		-	-	

*For electronic industry for sales less than $50 million.

Financial Operating Characteristics

	Industry			Company		
	19__	19__	19__	19__	19__	19__
Assets						
Accts & notes receiv.						
Inventory						
Total current						
Fixed current (net)						
TOTAL ASSETS						
Liabilities						
Accts & note payable						
Total current						
Long-term debt						
Net worth						
TOTAL LIAB.& NET WORTH						
Income						
Net sales						
Cost of goods sold						
Gross profit						
Operating expenses						
Operating profit						
Other expenses (net)						
PROFIT BEFORE TAXES						
Ratios						
Current						
Total debt/total asset						
T debt/tang. net worth						
Collection period days						
Net sales/inventory						
Total assets turnover						
Gross profit margin						
Operating profit marg.						
Return on net worth						

Financial Ratios

Liquidity Ratios

General Purpose

To measure the firm's ability to meet its current obligations as they come due.

To indicate the degree to which a firm is in a cash or near-cash position.

To measure the relationship between the supply of and the demand for cash assets.

Computation of Liquidity Ratios

$$\text{*Current Ratio} = \frac{\text{Current Assets}}{\text{Current Debt}}$$

Shows the firm's margin of safety with regard to meeting current debts from the current assets.

$$\text{Quick Ratio} = \frac{\text{Current Assest - Inventories}}{\text{Current Debt}}$$

Indicates the firm's ability to meet its current debts without relying upon inventory, which is the least liquid of a firm's current assets.

$$\text{*Inventory to Net Working Capital} = \frac{\text{Inventory}}{\text{Net Working Capital}}$$

An additional measure of inventory balance. If an excessive percentage of net working capital is reflected by unsold inventory, the firm may have difficulty in meeting currently maturing obligations.

$$\text{*Current Debt to Inventory} = \frac{\text{Current Debt}}{\text{Inventory}}$$

Another indication of the extent to which the firm relies on funds from disposal of unsold inventories to meet its current debts.

*One of Dun & Bradstreet's fourteen important operating and leverage ratios.

Leverage Ratios

General Purpose

Financial Structure Ratios

To compare the financing provided by owners with the financing provided by creditors.

To indicate the extent to which the firm relies on short-term and long-term borrowed funds.

Coverage Ratios

To measure the potential volatility of the firm's earnings due to the existence or introduction of fixed operating costs.

To measure the potential volatility of the firm's earnings due to the existence or introduction of fixed financial changes.

To measure the firm's ability to service fixed financial changes from current earnings.

Computation of Financial Structure Ratios

*Total Debt to Total Assets $= \dfrac{\text{Total Debt}}{\text{Total Assets}}$

Measures the firm's obligations to creditors in relation to the total funds supplied to the firm. Total debt includes current, intermediate-term, and long-term liabilities.

*Current Debt to Total Assets $= \dfrac{\text{Current Liabilities}}{\text{Total Assets}}$

Indicates the extent to which the firm relies on current debt to finance assets.

*Total Debt to Tangible Net Worth $= \dfrac{\text{Total Debt}}{\text{Tangible Net Worth}}$

When this relationship is high, a relatively small decrease in the value of assets could wipe out owner's equity and remove protection from creditors. Too much debt exposes the firm to the risks of unexpected contingencies and of being unable to borrow in case of need.

*Current Debt to Tangible New Worth $= \dfrac{\text{Current Debt}}{\text{Tangible Net Worth}}$

When this relationship is high, the firm is exposed to the hazards of frequent maturities, constant renewal problems, and perhaps the unavailability of short-term funds.

Computation of Coverage Ratios

Approximate Sales Volume Needed to Cover Operating Expenses $= \dfrac{\text{Fixed Operating Costs}}{1 - \left[\dfrac{\text{Variable Operating Costs}}{\text{Actual Net Sales}}\right]}$

Degree of Financial Leverage $= \dfrac{\text{Net Operating Profit}}{\text{Net Profit Before Taxes}}$

Measures the potential magnification of change in net return to common shareholders given a change in the level of operating profit.

Times Interest Earned $= \dfrac{\text{Net Profit Before Interest \& Taxes}}{\text{Interest Charges}}$

(The numerator is frequently referred to as EBIT—earnings before interest and taxes.)

Shows the relationship between earnings available for paying interest and interest charges. The ratio is closely related to degree of financial leverage. A low times interest earned means a high degree of financial leverage and vice versa.

Activity Ratios

General Purpose

To measure how effectively *assets* employed in the firm are being used. To measure how effectively *funds* employed in the firm are being used.

Computation of Efficiency Ratios

*Liquid Asset Turnover $= \dfrac{\text{Net Sales}}{\text{Cash + Marketable Securities}}$

Measures the firm's ability to control investment in cash and near-cash assets. Generally a high liquid asset velocity is desirable, since these assets produce zero or very small returns. However, a very high turnover may also incidate inadequate liquid assets and a potential liquidity problem.

*Receivables Turnover $= \dfrac{\text{Credit Sales}}{\text{Receivables}}$

Measures the firm's effectiveness in controlling investment in receivables. This ratio is particularly important for firms that sell mostly on a credit basis.

Collection Period Days $= \dfrac{\text{Notes and Accounts Receivable X 360}}{\text{Annual Credit Sales}}$

Used to analyze the collectibility of receivables. Generally, the collection period should not exceed the net maturity indicated by the terms of sale by more than one-third.

*Net Sales to Inventory $= \dfrac{\text{Net Sales}}{\text{Inventory}}$

(Also referred to as **Inventory Turnover**)

This ratio does not yield an actual physical turnover. It shows merely the relation of sales to inventory. A high ratio may indicate too little inventory. A low ratio may indicate too much. Cost of goods sold is often used instead of net sales to eliminate the effect of different price markups among the product lines of different firms.

*Total Asset Turnover $= \dfrac{\text{Net Sales}}{\text{Total Assets}}$

Used to measure the use of the total assets employed by the firm. This ratio measures the dollars of sales generated per dollar of investment in assets.

*Net Sales to Tangible Net Worth $= \dfrac{\text{Net Sales}}{\text{Tangible Net Worth}}$

(Also referred to as **Equity Turnover**)

If owner's equity turns over too slowly, funds become stagnant, and profitability suffers. If owner's equity turns over too fast, it may indicate that the amount owed to creditors has become a substitute for owner's funds.

Average Payment Period $= \dfrac{\text{Accounts Payable}}{\text{Credit Purchases}} \text{ X } \dfrac{\text{Number of Days}}{\text{in Period}}$

Indicates the average number of days the firm is taking to pay for credit purchases. This ratio is useful for comparing actual payments to terms of purchases.

Profitability Ratios

General Purpose

To measure management's overall effectiveness as shown by the returns generated on sales and investment.

Computation of Returns to Sales

$$\text{Gross Profit Margin} = \frac{\text{Gross Profit}}{\text{Net Sales}}$$

$$\text{Operating Profit Margin} = \frac{\text{Net Profit before Taxes}}{\text{Net Sales}}$$

$$\text{*Net Profit Margin after Taxes} = \frac{\text{Net Profit after Taxes}}{\text{Net Sales}}$$

Computation of Return on Asset Investment

$$\text{Return on Total Assets} = \frac{\text{Net Profit After Taxes}}{\text{Total Assets}}$$

$$\text{Return on Operating Assets} = \frac{\text{Operating Profit}}{\text{Operating Assets}}$$

Computation of Return on Owner's Investment

$$\text{Return on Net Worth} = \frac{\text{Net Profit after Taxes}}{\text{Net Worth}}$$

$$\text{*Return on Investment} = \frac{\text{Net Profit after Taxes}}{\text{Net Assets}}$$

$$\text{Dividend Yield} = \frac{\text{Dividends per Share of Common Stock}}{\text{Market Price per Share of Common Stock}}$$

$$\text{Earnings per Share of Common Stock} = \frac{\text{Net Profit After Taxes Less Preferred Stock Dividends}}{\text{Number of Outstanding Shares of Common Stock}}$$

$$\text{Price/Earnings Ratio} = \frac{\text{Market Price per Common Share}}{\text{Earnings per Common Share}}$$

Definitions Used in Computing Ratios

Average daily credit sales are obtained by dividing the credit sales made during a period by the number of days in the period.

Common equity is the common shareholder's investment, in the firm. It is measured by subtracting total debt and preferred stock from total assets. Common equity normally includes the common stock, paid-in surplus, and retained earnings accounts.

Contribution margin is the excess of net sales revenue over variable operating costs. It is so called because it represents the contribution of revenues to overhead (fixed operating expenses) and profit.

Current assets are cash resources or resources that can reasonably be expected to be turned into cash within either the firm's normal operating cycle or one year. Current assets include cash, marketable securities, notes and accounts receivable (less reserve for bad debts), inventory, and prepaid expenses.

Current debt is the total of all liabilities currently incurred that will be due and payable within one year.

Equity is the ownership interest in the firm. It is normally determined by subtracting total debt from total assets.

Fixed operating costs are operating expenses that tend to remain relatively unchanged as production and sales levels change. For many firms, expenses for supervisory salaries, depreciation, amortization, insurance and other types of overhead requirements do not vary directly with the level of production but tend to remain relatively constant within capacity constraints.

Funded debt is the total of all long-term obligations, as represented by mortgages, bonds, debentures, term loans, and other types of liabilities maturing more than one year from the date of the financial statement.

Gross profit is net sales minus cost of goods sold.

Liquid assets are the cash and near-cash assets of the firm. Near-cash assets normally include highly marketable money market instruments.

Net Assets are total assets minus current liabilities.

Net sales are obtained by subtracting sales returns and allowances and cash discounts taken on sales from gross sales.

Net working capital is the excess of current assets over current debt. It is obtained by subtracting total current debt from total current assets.

Operating assets are those assets which the firm needs to carry out its normal activities. They are obtained by subtracting nonoperating assets, such as unrelated securities, real estate, and intangible assets, from total assets.

Operating profit is net sales minus all related operating expenses including cost of goods sold, general and administrative expenses, and selling expenses.

Quick assets are total current assets minus inventory.

Tangible net worth is owners', partners', or stockholders' equity in the business. It is obtained by subtracting total debt from total assets and then deducting the dollar amount of intangible assets carried by the firm.

Total debt is the sum of all current and long-term liabilities.

Variable operating costs are those expenses, such as direct labor and direct material, which tend to vary directly with the level of production and sales.

MARKET ANALYSIS

Market Scope and Market Distribution

What is the geographic distribution of your industry's market? To answer this question, you will need to consider two things:

Market scope. Market scope may be local, regional, national, or international. Describe the scope of your company's market.

Market distribution. If the market is not local, describe the distribution methods used in the industry.

```
Market Scope and Market Distribution




















```

Market Segmentation

A market segment is a group of the industry's customers who share a set of common characteristics that distinguish them from other customers. Often different marketing approaches are required to reach different segments. Most segments share one or more of the following characteristics:

Geography
    Region
    County size
    City size
    Density
    Climate

Demographics
    Age
    Sex
    Family size and status
    Income
    Occupation
    Education
    Religion or culture
    Social class

Psychographics
    Life style
    Personality
    Purchase occasion
    Benefits sought
    Usage rate
    Degree of loyalty
    Sensitivity factor

Different market segments may require different product or service characteristics (features, sizes, packages). Or they may require different distribution channels, promotion methods, or sales terms. However, these differences are not so great that the different segments must be served by different industries. To the extent possible, describe the characteristics of your company's market segments.

Market Segmentation

Market Demand Changes and Trends

Describe any significant changes that have occurred in the market demand in the past few years. Describe any trends that point to future changes. Possible changes include:

o Changes in the relative size of market demand

o Changes in the geographic distribution of the market

o The emergence of new segments or the disappearance of old ones

Market Demand Changes and Trends

Major Customers and Concentration

Describe the principal types of customers served by your industry and the key characteristics of those customers. Define your customers clearly. List some actual and potential customers for your product or service. Explain who the major purchasers are and rank them by the percentage of sales each represents.

The major customer categories are:

o Consumers: age, income, family size, proximity

o Companies: size, type, ownership (independent or franchise operation)

o Industry: size, type, ownership

o Government: local, state, federal

Major Customers and Concentration

Sales Tactics

Describe the method you use or intend to use to sell your product or service. Will you use your own sales force, sales representatives, distributors, or retailers? Compare your established margins and commissions to those of your competitors. Describe any special policies regarding discounts and exclusive distribution rights. Indicate the company's normal sales terms. What percentage of sales are made for cash or credit? What discounts are offered for rapid payment?

Sales Tactics

Distribution Channels

In today's small world, most suppliers and producers do not sell their company's goods directly to the final users. Between the company and the final user stand a variety of middlemen (distributors, retailers, and so on.) Describe your company's inflow and outflow channels of distribution. To what degree do you depend on middlemen?

Distribution Channels

Pricing Trends

Pricing policy is very important. The price must be right to penetrate the market, maintain market position, and produce the profits. What trends in pricing for your major products or services have occurred in the past three years? Have your prices been rising faster or more slowly than the overall inflation rate?

Pricing Trends

Promotion and Advertising

What are your company's advertising channels? What are your advertising and promotion costs? Advertising channels include direct mail, publications, and other types of media. Products and services may be advertised on an individual basis or cooperatively, as when a manufacturer and retailer share the cost of local advertising.

Advertising and promotion costs are best figured as a percentage of sales or revenues. Sources of industry information include trade associations and trade publications; advertising agencies and associations, and advertising industry publications. Has the ratio of advertising costs to sales been increasing or decreasing over the past three years?

Promotion and Advertising

Major Competitors

Use the chart entitled COMPETITOR PROFILE to complete your competition profile. This profile presents key information about your market competitors. You can use it to determine your company's relative competitive position. You can also use it to identify possible strategic responses to your competitors' actions.

In completing the profile, include information about each major competitor and any potential competitors. When competitors are large corporations, identify which part of the corporation you are competing with.

Rank your major competitors by sales volume. For each one, specify:

Sales volume. To find each competitor's sales volume, you need to use published information, if available, or your own estimate of sales. Documents such as annual reports, trade association publications, and others are extremely useful for this purpose.

Growth rate. Based on a particular industry average, indicate if the growth rate for each competitor is high, medium, low, unchanged, or declining.

Degree of integration. Indicate whether your competitors are forward or backward integrated and to what degree.

Strengths and weaknesses. Make a realistic assessment of your competitors' strengths and weaknesses. Consider individual products and services. List the things that your competitors do particularly poorly or particularly well. Include both objective measures (lower purchasing costs, outdated production equipment) and subjective measures (a reputation for high quality or for poorly trained service personnel).

Total sales volume and average growth rate. From your experience, is each competitor's average growth rate, higher than, the same as, or lower than the industry growth rate?

Competitor's market share. What percentage of the market does your competitor command? Base this estimate on your own assessment of your competitors and their products. (This estimate should be translated to total market size and compared to industry size.) To find industry size, refer to your calculations in the section entitled, INDUSTRY ANALYSIS.

COMPETITOR PROFILE

Major Competitors	Sales Volume ($000)	Growth Rate	Degree of Integration	Strengths	Weaknesses
AB Industries	1,000	20%	N/A	None	Marketing and under capitalization
Net-First	3,000	50%	N/A	Product technology Cash reserve Marketing	None
Best Cat	15,000	35%	Backward	Strong marketing team	Quality of product is poor
Total sales volume of major competitors and average growth rate	19,000	36.6%			
Competitor's market share	30%'				
Industry market share	63,333				

COMPETITOR PROFILE

Major Competitors	Sales Volume ($000)	Growth Rate	Degree of Integration	Strengths	Weaknesses
Total sales volume of major competitors and average growth rate					
Competitor's market share					
Industry market share					

Market Share and Sales

What market share of the total industry size does your company represent? This market share should be translated to forecast market sales. Estimate in units and dollars the market sales that your company can achieve. (Market sales are the estimated sales to a specified customer base in a specified geographical area within a specified period.) Base this estimate on your assessment of your customers and their acceptance of your product or service; the size of your market; trends in the market; and the competition. Market sales estimates should be monthly for the next fiscal year and yearly for the next three years. For management visibility plot your forecast sales on the charts: *FORECAST MONTHLY SALES* and *FORECAST YEAR-TO-DATE SALES* for management visability. Sample of forecast monthly and year-to-date sales are illustrated for your convenience. The growth of your sales should be related to the industry growth rate. That is if the industry is growing at an annual rate of 15 percent, then your company's growth rate should be approximately the same.

Market Share and Sales

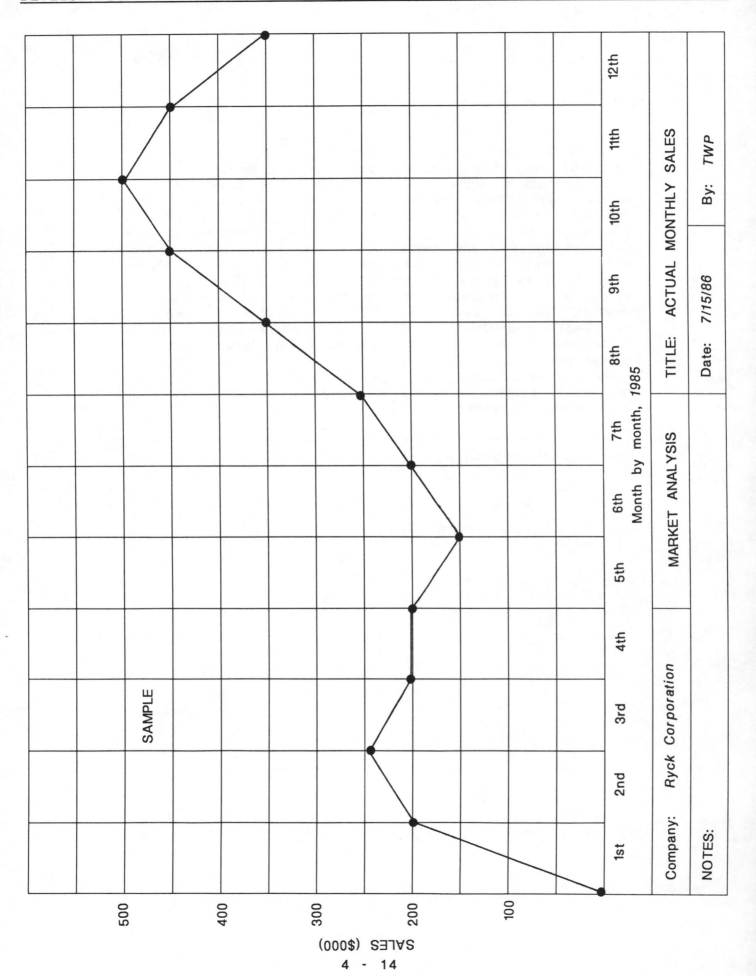

SAMPLE

Month by month, 1985

SALES ($000)

Company:	Ryck Corporation	MARKET ANALYSIS	TITLE: ACTUAL MONTHLY SALES
NOTES:			Date: 7/15/86	By: TWP

	1st	2nd	3rd	4th	5th	6th	7th	8th	9th	10th	11th	12th

Month by month, 19

SALES ($000)

MARKET ANALYSIS

TITLE:

Company:

Date:

By:

NOTES:

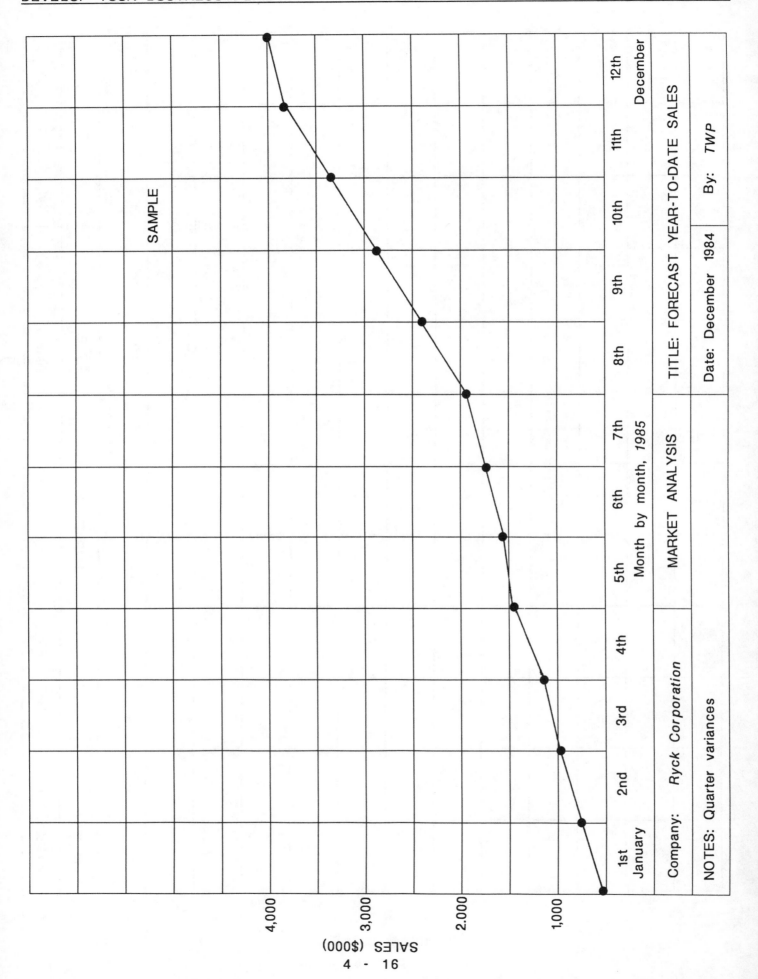

SAMPLE

SALES ($000)

4,000

3,000

2,000

1,000

1st
January

2nd

3rd

4th

5th

6th
Month by month, 1985

7th

8th

9th

10th

11th

12th
December

Company: Ryck Corporation

MARKET ANALYSIS

TITLE: FORECAST YEAR-TO-DATE SALES

NOTES: Quarter variances

Date: December 1984

By: TWP

1st	2nd	3rd	4th	5th	6th	7th	8th	9th	10th	11th	12th

Company: | MARKET ANALYSIS | TITLE:

NOTES: | Date: | By:

SALES ($000)

STRATEGIC PLANNING

Long-Term Goals

List the company's long-term goals. Describe what you plan to achieve within a designated time period. Examples would be sales, employment, or product goals. The goals should be based on the development of strategies in the business plan, rather than on dreams or hopes. However, they may be goals that can not be achieved within the period covered by the current plan.

Long-Term Goals

Key Performance Indicators

Key performance indicators are financial and nonfinancial performance measures that are used to track the company's progress toward achieving goals. They include profitability, number of employees, and net asset value. Remember that those measures relate to overall goals rather than to specific strategies. Use the chart on the following page to list your company's long-term goals and key performance indicators. For example:

o A retailer who is attempting to grow by developing his product line should list as key performance indicators sales revenue, number of new products, advertising and promotion expenses, and selling expenses as a percentage of sales.

o A manufacturing company that is trying to enhance its image as a quality producer by improving its technology should list as its performance indicators: research and development costs, number of new engineering and quality control staff, and expenses for advertising aimed at promoting that quality image.

Key Performance Indicators						
			Future Years			
	Last Year	This Year	1986	1987	1988	1989
Revenues ($000)	1000	1200	4000	9000	18000	30000
Net income after taxes ($000)	(400)	0	280	1000	2160	4500
Return on sales (%)	-	-	7	10	12	15
Return on net investment (%)	-	-	10	20	30	40
Number of employees (count)	8	12	35	60	90	165
Percent growth /year in sales	-	20	233	125	100	67

Key Performance Indicators						
		Future Years				
	Last Year	This Year	19___	19___	19___	19___
Revenues ($000)						
Net income after taxes ($000)						
Return on sales (%)						
Return on net assets (%)						
Number of employees (count)						

Milestone Schedule

You will need to make out a milestone schedule that shows the timing of and the responsibility for the activities that are necessary to realize your company's objectives. A well-prepared schedule will show critical deadlines and can be used to raise money. In addition, the schedule will demonstrate to potential investors that management knows how to plan and how to minimize risk.

The month-by-month milestones should show such activities as product development, market planning, hiring, and the addition of new equipment. Use the *MILESTONE SCHEDULE* provided to schedule critical deadlines and essential activities. For example, milestones for a new venture could include:

√ Incorporation of the venture
√ Funding of the venture
√ Completion of the prototype
√ Sales representative agreement
√ Trade show displays
√ Distributor and dealer agreement
√ Placement of material orders
√ Start of the operation
√ Receipt of first orders
√ First sales and deliveries
√ Receipt of first accounts receivable

1986 MILESTONE SCHEDULE

XYZ Corporation

PAGE __1__ of __1__

Legend

	Start	Order	Receive	Release	Bar
Milestones					Plan
	△	☐	☆	—∞	
Actual	▲	■	★	••	Actual
	Complete	Assemble	Finish		

Milestone Description	Jan Feb Mar Apr May Jun Jul Aug Sep Oct Nov Dec	Remarks
Business Plan		complete 11/85
Incorporation		complete 3/84
Key Management		founders 12/84
Corporate Advisers		
Office Set-up		
Prototype		
Funding (1st round)		$500,000
Product #1		
Production Start		
Advertising		2 magazines
First shipment		
Product #2		

MILESTONE SCHEDULE

Legend

Milestones: Start, Order, Receive, Release

Actual: Complete, Assemble, Finish

Bar: Plan, Actual

PAGE ____ of ____

Milestone Description		Remarks

Plan Assumptions

Plan assumptions are the expected external conditions under which the company will execute its plan. List the conditions that are most important to your industry and the trends that you expect during the period covered by the plan. Try hard to make good estimates, don't worry if your assumptions turn out not to be perfectly accurate. You are listing them so that you will know when your plan needs to be revised. If you fail to list your assumptions, you may miss an important external change. Plan assumptions fall into four categories:

Economy. List economic conditions that are relevant to your company. These conditions may include overall economic growth, general inflation, specific price trends, wage rates, interest rates, and so on. Sources for this information include government agencies, general business publications, and the larger banks. The banks constitute the best sources; most of them make economic projections for major geographical areas and for the most important industries in their state.

Industry. List industry trends. Include such projections as capacity growth and status, new technologies, and changes in your company's competitive position.

Market. List market trends. Include expected changes in demand for your product or service; changes in market distribution (by geographic area or by types of customers); changes in customer needs or wants; and competitors' actions in the marketplace (for example, aggressive pricing or the introduction of a new product).

Outside influences. Government or other regulatory actions are important outside influences. Outside influences may also include changing technology not directly related to your business. List these and anything else that is important to your company and that does not fit into the previous categories.

Plan Assumptions
Economy
Industry
Market
Outside Influences

Red Flags

Red flags are problems that cannot be resolved in the process of completing the business plan or items that you will need to examine again later. Red flags may be resolved within the near future by conducting market or product research or seeking advice from a consultant or an accountant.

Red Flags

STRATEGIC OPPORTUNITIES

Company Strengths to Exploit

Company strengths were identified in the *Company Analysis* section. Before you select your strategies, it is important to review your company's major strengths and determine how you can exploit them to help your company grow.

Company Strengths to Exploit

Company Weaknesses to Overcome

Company weaknesses were also identified in the *Company Analysis* section and should also be reviewed before you select your strategies. The small electronics firm in our example may find that its principal weakness is meeting product delivery dates. It might correct the problem by purchasing better raw materials, improving production control, improving its system for estimating delivery dates and filling orders.

Company Weaknesses to Overcome

Market Opportunities to Exploit

Market segments served by your company and by the industry as a whole were described in the previous section. Before you select your strategies, identify markets that are not currently served by your company or even by your industry. For example, many small businesses service one small geographic area. Other geographic areas might offer a new opportunity. For another business, different types of customers might offer a new opportunity.

Market Opportunities to Exploit

Risk Analysis

Risks are conditions that may prevent a company from achieving its objectives. Before you select your strategies, identify areas in which the company's risks should be minimized. Risks can be found in all areas of a business, but small businesses are most vulnerable to financial risk. Specific problems include undercapitalization, inefficient collection practices, and insufficient reserves to cover emergencies.

Use the chart entitled *RISK ANALYSIS* to identify your important risks. Merely indicate your company's level of risk associates with each risk element. Mark an X to indicate low, medium, or high risk. The overall level of risk is assigned to the column in which most of the elements fall.

Risk Analysis			
Element	**Ratings**		
	Low	Medium	High
Industry	X		
Market			X
Competitive position		X	
Strategy		X	
Assumptions	X		
Financial performance	X		
Management performance		X	
Level of future performance	X		
Others			
Overall risk		X	

Risk Analysis			
Element	Ratings		
	Low	Medium	High
Industry			
Market			
Competitive position			
Strategy			
Assumptions			
Financial performance			
Management performance			
Level of future performance			
Others			
Overall risk			

Business Strategies

Use the chart entitled *BUSINESS STRATEGIES* to list possible business strategies for your company. In the first column, indicate with an X which strategies your company is currently pursuing. In the second column, indicate which strategies your company might want to pursue in the future. In the third column, indicate briefly how you might implement the future strategies. For example; a company that manufactures electronic connectors might select:

o **Market Rationalization.** Tactic: cut back national sales effort to focus on the Sunbelt.

o **Product Line Development.** Tactic: begin making multiconnect switches.

o **Technology Focus.** Tactic: use unique gold connector on all switches.

o **Operations Capability Expansion.** Tactic: add second shift in plant.

Note that the strategies are grouped into six categories. You may choose to focus on strategies in all or any one of these categories. The six categories are described briefly below. They are described in more detail later in this section.

Market strategies. Market strategies are actions a company may take to create and maintain demand for its products or services. The key concept in market strategy is market share.

Product line strategies. Product line strategies are actions a company may take with respect to the composition and positioning of its product lines. The key concept here is product line. A **product line** is a *family* of related products or services.

Technology strategies. Technology strategies deal with the extent to which a company emphasizes technology as a major competitive factor. The key concept is that every industry has a technology related to its processes, equipment, and products or services.

Operations strategies. Operations strategies are the actions a company may take to perform the actual functions related to production or performance of a service. They focus on capacity, processes, and quality control.

Retrenchment strategies. Retrenchment strategies are corrective actions a company may take when it finds itself in financial or competitive trouble. The idea is to reduce risk and exposure until decisions can be made about the company's future. Retrenchment is **not** a long-term option; it must lead either to correcting the company's problems or to closing the company.

Financial strategies. Financial strategies are actions a company may take to provide capital for ongoing operations and growth. This capital may be equity or business debt in the form of loans.

Business Strategies			
	Present Strategy	Future Strategy	Tactics
Market strategies			
Market Position Enhancement	✓	✓	reduced price
Development of New Markets		✓	inter-national
Market Rationalization			
Licensing			
Produce line strategies			
Product Line Enhancement			
Product Line Development		✓	pig-back products
Product Line Rationalization			
Technology Strategies			
Focus	✓	✓	emerging tech.
Operations Strategies			
Capability Expansion	✓		
Capability Reduction			
Operations Improvement		✓	capital equip.
Quality Adjustment			
Distribution Improvement			
Human Resources Enhancement			
Retrenchment Strategies			
Hesitation			
General Cost Cutting			
Financial Strategies			
Financial Mix Adjustment			
External Financing	✓		venture capital
Going Public			
Seeking a Buyer			

Business Strategies			
	Present Strategy	Future Strategy	Tactics
Market strategies			
Market Position Enhancement			
Development of New Markets			
Market Rationalization			
Licensing			
Produce line strategies			
Product Line Enhancement			
Product Line Development			
Product Line Rationalization			
Technology Strategies			
Focus			
Operations Strategies			
Capability Expansion			
Capability Reduction			
Operations Improvement			
Quality Adjustment			
Distribution Improvement			
Human Resources Enhancement			
Retrenchment Strategies			
Hesitation			
General Cost Cutting			
Financial Strategies			
Financial Mix Adjustment			
External Financing			
Going Public			
Seeking a Buyer			

Company Thrusts and Business Strategies

A **company thrust** describes the overall direction in which the company is going. It may also describe the expected outcome of the business plan. The direction or expected outcome may be fast growth, differentiation, or turnaround. Each company thrust is supported by a group of **business strategies**. These strategies describe actions for each area of the business. See the chart entitled *COMPANY THRUSTS AND BUSINESS STRATEGIES*. Once you have chosen a thrust for your company and a group of strategies to support that thrust, you can develop your **strategy plan**. This strategy plan will be based on your company's objectives, opportunities, strengths, weaknesses, and competitive position. It will describe the tactics that you will use to implement your business plan.

Company thrusts are described in detail later in this section. At this point you only need to know that each company thrust is appropriate to business in certain stages of maturity or in certain competitive positions. See the chart entitled *GUIDE TO COMPANY THRUSTS*. Using this chart as a reference, list the appropriate company thrust for your company.

GUIDE TO COMPANY THRUSTS				
Competitive Position	Embryonic	Growth	Mature	Aging
Strong	Start-up Differen- tiate Fast Grow	Fast Grow Differen- tiate Grow/w Industry	Focus/ Develop Niche Differen- tiate Grow w/ Industry	Focus/ Develop Niche Different- iate Retrench
Average	Start-up Differen- titate Focus/ Develop Niche Fast Grow	Differen- tiate Focus/ Develop Niche Renew Grow/w Industry	Renew Focus/ Develop Niche Differen- titate Grow/w Industry	Renew Retrench
Weak	Focus/ Develop Niche Fast Grow Renew	Focus/ Develop Niche Differen- tiate Grow w/ Industry	Retrench	Withdraw

COMPANY THRUSTS AND BUSINESS STRATEGIES

Business Strategies	Start-up	Grow with Industry	Fast Grow	Focus/Develop Niche	Differentiate	Renew	Hang in	Retrench
Market strategies								
Market Position Enhancement	✓	✓	✓	✓	✓	✓		
Development of New Markets	✓	✓	✓	✓				
Market Rationalization			✓	✓	✓	✓	✓	✓
Licensing		✓					✓	
Product line strategies								
Product Line Enhancement		✓		✓		✓	✓	
Product Line Development	✓		✓			✓		
Product Line Rationalization			✓	✓	✓	✓	✓	✓
Technology strategies								
Technology Focus	✓	✓	✓	✓	✓	✓	✓	✓
Operations strategies								
Operations Capability Expansion	✓	✓	✓	✓				
Operations Capability Reduction							✓	✓
Operations Improvement		✓	✓	✓	✓	✓	✓	
Quality Adjustment				✓	✓	✓		
Distribution Improvement		✓	✓	✓		✓		
Human Resources Enhamcement						✓	✓	
Retrenchment Strategies								
Hesitation								
General Cost Cutting		✓						
Financial strategies								
Financial Mix Adjustment		✓		✓	✓	✓		
External Financing	✓	✓	✓			✓		
Going Public		✓	✓					
Seeking a Buyer		✓	✓				✓	✓

Strategy Plan

Now you are ready to develop your strategy plan. Use the chart on the following page. In completing each section, consider the definitions presented below:

Thrust and Strategies. You have already identified the strengths and weaknesses of your company. Based on this assessment and on your company's goals, list the company thrust and the business strategies that you believe will ensure the survival and growth of your business. See the following pages for detailed definitions of the various thrusts and strategies.

Tactics. Identify the tactics with which you intend to implement each strategy.

Timing. Specify the time frame within which the tactics will be implemented. For example, if you are pursuing a loan, a reasonable time frame might be three months.

Responsibility. Name the individual who will be primarily responsible for implementing each tactic.

Estimated Costs. List the monetary and nonmonetary costs of pursuing each tactic.

Source of Funds. If there are monetary costs associated with a tactic, specify where the necessary funds will come from.

Strategy Plan
Thrust
Strategies
Tactics
Timing
Responsibility
Estimated Costs
Source of Funds

Company Thrusts Description

Start-up
Grow with Industry
Fast Grow
Focus/Develop Niche
Differentiate
Renew
Hang in
Retrench

START-UP

Definition

To introduce a new product or service with clear, significant technology breakthrough

Objective

To develop a totally new industry and satisfy demand where none existed before

Requirements

Risk-taking attitude on the part of management, capital expenditures, expense

Expected Results

Negative cash flow, low to negative returns, a leadership position in new industry

Risks

High to very high; demand, technology, channels of distribution, sourcing, basis of competition all unknown

Natural Period of Execution

Embryonic

Typical Strategies

Market Position Enhancement
Development of New Markets
Technology Focus
External Financing

5 - 22

GROW WITH INDUSTRY

Definition

To limit efforts to those necessary to maintain market share and to ensure a stable competitive position.

Objective

To free resources to correct weaknesses in market, product, management, or production

Requirements

Restraint on the part of management, market intelligence, some capital and expense investments, time-limited strategy

Expected Results

Stable market share; profit, cash flow, and return on net assets not significantly worse than recent history, and fluctuating only with industry averages

Risks

Medium to high in strenuously competitive industries essentially; a defensive posture

Natural Period of Execution

Embryonic, Growth, Mature, Aging

Typical Strategies

Market Position Enhancement
Product Line Enhancement
Product Line Development
Operations Capability Expansion
Financial Mix Adjustment

FAST GROW

Definition

To pursue aggressively a larger market share or a stronger competitive position or both

Objective

To increase volume and share faster than competition and faster than general industry growth rate

Requirements

Available resources for investment and follow-up, risk-taking attitude on the part of management, an appropriate investment strategy

Expected Results

Greater market share; in the short term, perhaps lower returns; above-average returns in longer term; competitive retaliation

Risks

High; threat of someone else playing the game smarter, harder, or sooner

**Natural Period
of Execution**

Embryonic, Growth, Mature

Typical Strategies

Market Position Enhancement
Development of New Markets
Technology Focus
Operations Capability Expansion
Distribution Improvement
External Financing
Going Public

FOCUS/DEVELOP NICHE

Definition

To select and protect a particular segment of the market or a particular product line narrower in scope than those of competing firms

Objective

To serve the strategic target area (geographic, product, or market) more efficiently, more fully, and more profitably than it can be served by broad-line competitors

Requirements

Disciplined management, persistent pursuit of well-defined scope and mission, premium pricing, careful selection of targets

Expected Results

Above-average earnings, possibility of being low-cost producer in area, possibility of attaining high differentiation

Risks

Medium; danger of selecting a poor segment or of failing to sustain efforts over long enough period

Natural Period of Execution

Embryonic, Growth, Mature, Aging

Typical Strategies

Market Position Development
Development of New Markets
Product Line Development
Operations Improvement
Technology Focus

DIFFERENTIATE

Definition

To achieve what customer perceives as the most distinctive quality or service in the industry that is consistent with acceptable costs

Objective

To insulate the company from switching, substitution, price competition, and loss of loyal customers or suppliers to the competition

Requirements

Willingness to sacrifice high market share, careful target marketing, focused technological and market research, strong brand loyalty

Expected Results

Possibly lowered market share, high margins, above-average earnings, highly defensible position

Risks

Medium; requires company to select a posture not easy for competitors to duplicate

Natural Period of Execution

Embryonic, Growth, Mature

Typical Strategies

Market Position Enhancement
Market Rationalization
Product Line Rationalization
Operations Improvement
Quality Adjustment

RENEW

Definition

To overcome severe weakness and restore the competitiveness of a product line in anticipation of future industry sales

Objectives

To overcome weakness in product-market mix in order to improve share; or to prepare for a new generation of demand, competition, or substitute products

Requirements

Strong enough competitive position to generate necessary resources for renewal efforts, capital and expense investments, management capable of taking risk, recognition of potential threats to existing line

Expected Results

Short-term decline in sales, then sudden or gradual breaking away of old volume-profit patterns

Risks

Medium to high; entails many of the same threats as new product and new market strategies, compounded by greater maturity of industry

Natural Period of Execution

Growth, Mature, Aging

Typical Strategies

Market Position Enhancement
Product Line Rationalization
Operations Improvement
Quality Adjustment
External Financing

HANG IN

Definition

To prolong existence of the
company in anticipation of some
specific favorable change in the
environment

Objective

To continue operating a weak
company only long enough to take
advantage of unusual opportunity
known to be at hand; this might
take the form of the expiration
of a patent, a change in management
or a technological breakthrough

Requirements

Clear view of expected environmental
shifts, a management willing and
able to sustain poor performance,
opportunity and resources to
capitalize on new environment, a
time limit

Expected Results

Poorer than average performance,
perhaps losses; later, substantial
growth and high returns

Risks

High; the future never comes as
fast or turns out to be as favorable
as a weak company expects; stronger
competitors will probably benefit
most anyway

**Natural Period
of Execution**

Growth, Mature, Aging

Typical Strategies

Market Rationalization
Product Line Rationalization
Operations Improvement
Hesitation
General Cost Cutting

RETRENCH

Definition

To cut back investment in the company or to sell product line or operations resources so as to reduce level of risk and exposure to losses and free up capital

Objective

To stop unacceptable losses or risks, to prepare the company for sale or withdrawal, to strip away loss operations

Requirements

Highly disciplined management system, good communication with employees to prevent wholesale departures, clear strategic objective and timetable

Expected Results

Reduced losses or modestly improved performance

Risks

Low to medium; performance may be predictable but not acceptable

Natural Period of Execution

Growth, Mature, Aging

Typical Strategies

Market Rationalization
Product Line Rationalizaiton
Operations Capability Reduction
General Cost Cutting
Seeking a Buyer

BUSINESS STRATEGIES DESCRIPTION

Market Strategies

Market Position Enhancement
Development of New Markets
Market Rationalization
Licensing

Product Line Strategies

Product Line Enhancement
Product Line Development
Product Line Rationalization

Technology Strategies

Technology Focus

Operations Strategies

Operations Capability Expansion
Operations Capability Relduction
Operations Improvement
Quality Adjustment
Distribution Improvement
Human Resources Enhancement

Retrenchment Strategies

Hesitation
General Cost Cutting

Financial Strategies

Financial Mix Adjustment
External Financing
Going Public
Seeking a Buyer

MARKET STRATEGIES

Market Position Enhancement

The **focus** may be on existing position or on new products, services, or markets. The **objective** is to increase market share either by taking customers away from competitors or by capturing a larger share of market growth. **Tactics** entail significant spending on marketing practices and activities. They may include improving the product or service by restyling or repackaging; repositioning the product or service; pricing aggressively, or mounting a major advertising campaign. For example:

A supermarket advertises low prices, issues discount coupons in local newspapers, and sets and promotes extremely low sale prices for a few items in order to attract customers.

Development of New Markets

The **focus** is on expanding the number or scope of markets for an existing product or service. The **objective** is to increase the size of the market. Sometimes exporting is used to offset a declining domestic market. Exporting is generally an option for manufacturers. There are export opportunities in some service businesses (banking, hotel management, insurance) and in construction, but these opportunities are generally available only to the largest firms in the industry. Export opportunities exist in wholesale and retail trade through mail order operations, particularly for companies with a unique product or a special image.

Tactics include acquisition or setting up a plant, store, or service outlet in another country. These tactics are almost always reserved for larger companies such as Sears, IBM, and McDonalds. The actual acquisition of another company is rarely an option available to small businesses, although occasionally a retailer may purchase a competitor and use the location and inventory to expand its own usiness. However, joint venture and sub-contract arrangements are frequently used by small businesses in such industries as construction and consulting, when the small business may bring added manpower and/or special skills to a larger firm, or a consortium of small businesses may join to win contracts that none of them could undertake alone.

Market Rationalization

The **objective** is to focus marketing effort on the most profitable, or potentially profitable, markets or segments in order to earn a higher return on each marketing dollar. **Tactics** include concentrating on high-margin or high-volume markets; using the highest-volume distributors; limiting the customers served—through minimum-volume requirements or a volume-based price structure; and practicing selective abandonment of certain market segments. For example:

o A clothing manufacturer sets a minimum order of 1,000 wool shirts. In addition, it structures prices so as to make orders of less than 3,000 units very unattractive on a unit cost basis. As a result, small clothing stores are effectively shut out.

o A construction firm decides to stop bidding on government work and to concentrate on the commercial-industrial market because it obtains lower margins on government jobs and finds the bidding process cumbersome and expensive.

o It is common in the travel industry for tour operators to set up special incentive programs that pay higher commissions to the travel agencies that generate significant volume. Agencies that sell only one or two packages a year receive a much smaller commission.

Licensing

This strategy is adopted by small businesses that develop a new idea but do not have and cannot raise the capital they need to bring it to market.

The **objective** may be to reduce capital requirements (and associated risks) as well as to realize additional earnings. **Tactics** include licensing product formulas to other companies, selling rights to the use of the brand name, selling process know-how, and combining all of the foregoing tactics in a franchise operation. For example:

o A construction and engineering firm licenses the design it has developed for a passive solar house

o A fast-food outlet sells a franchise based on its name, menu concept, and decor.

o A national car rental company sells individual local agencies the right to use its name. It backs the licensees with national advertising and a computerized data base and it finances the purchase of the licensees' fleets.

PRODUCT LINE STRATEGIES

Product Line Enhancement

The **objective** is to keep pace with the industry as a whole with respect to the features, styles, and quality of products or services. **Tactics** include major or minor redesign, incorporation of new technology, repackaging, and normal replacement. For example:

o During the 1970's, innumerable products were rejuvenated by substituting electronic components for mechanical or electromechanical components. Among these products were adding machines (replaced by calculators, often hand-held), watches, office machines (electronic typewriters), and telephone switching equipment.

o After the fluorocarbon scare of the late 1970's, most manufacturers of health and beauty aids repackaged their products in nonaerosol spray forms.

o Banks and savings institutions were given the option of offering interest-bearing checking accounts at the beginning of 1981. This immediately became the standard for the industry. A year later, every institution was providing this same service, albeit with somewhat different features.

Product Line Development

The **objective** is to increase revenues by selling new products, by selling old products with new features, by broadening the range of new products and by finding new uses for existing products. **Tactics** include introduction selling of the concept of, or the need for, the new product; extensive promotion of the new product, often accompanied by introductory prices and trial samples; filling gaps in the existing product line (adding sizes, styles or varieties); acquiring a company with a complementary product line; and contracting for the supply of a complementary product line from a domestic or foreign source to be sold under your name. For example:

o A manufacturer of traditional toys and games adds a line of electronic products aimed at the adult market.

o A construction contractor whose business is residential and commercial painting and wallpapering adds staff to perform tile, carpet, and hardwood floor installation so that it can provide a complete interior finishing service.

o Retailers contract for many kinds of merchandise (applicances, food products, apparel) that can be sold under the store's name (or other private label), usually in order to offer a low or moderately priced product line.

Product Line Rationalization

The **objective** is to focus the company's efforts and resources on the most profitable products and services. **Tactics** include product line and packaging standardization, product repositioning, and the selective abandonment of unprofitable or marginal products. For example:

o Auto manufacturers are redesigning their models to use standard-ized parts, in order to reduce inventories and provide more flexibility to change the mix of products offered.

o An electrical contractor with a broad range of services might choose to abandon residential repair services and concentrate on major new construction and rehabilitation jobs. His reasoning might be that a low volume of high priced residential service work did not justify the additional paperwork and scheduling problems it entailed.

o A small suburban paint and wallpaper store might choose to stop carrying certain wallpaper patterns that sold poorly.

TECHNOLOGY STRATEGIES

Technology Focus

This strategy emphasizes exploiting or acquiring new technology or ensuring that the company keeps pace with technologies currently used in the industry.

Depending on the business, the **objective** is to establish an image as a leader or a specialist in order to support market or operations strategies. **Tactics** include investment in basic research, monitoring relevant emerging technologies in the industry and in other industries, investigating new applications for the company's main technologies, and purchasing patent rights and licenses. For example:

o Tandem Computers built its company on systems that incorporate duplicate processors. These processors are intended for users who cannot afford to have their computers *go down*.

o McDonald's achieved its early success by taking advantage of systems which permitted precision food preparation. This enabled McDonald's to provide rapid service and a consistent product in all of its outlets.

o Federal Express was following a strategy of technology focus when it established a small-package delivery service based on its own fleet of planes and a central sorting and distribution operation.

OPERATIONS STRATEGIES

Operations Capability Expansion

The **objective** is to increase output and revenues derived from the company's existing physical and staff resources, or to increase the resources available to meet demand. **Tactics** include investing in additional facilities, equipment, and inventories beyond normal replacement needs; changing in physical or operating systems to eliminate bottlenecks; improving processes and procedures; and hiring additional employees. For example:

o Manufacturers routinely build or buy new plants, add production lines to existing plants, and add second shifts in plants that previously supported a single shift. The electronics industry has been doing this for years, although economic conditions slowed its expansion somewhat in 1982. Many manufacturers have shifted some or all of their capacity overseas to take advantage of cheap foreign labor.

o Construction contractors often employ a permanent staff of craftsmen to handle the normal workload, and hire additional workers to meet increased demand on specific projects.

Operations Capability Reduction

The **objective** is usually to respond to a decrease in current or expected future demand caused by market saturation or the introduction of substitute products or services. In some cases, this strategy may be used to improve the economics of the business by reducing size while increasing efficiency and profits. **Tactics** include reducing shift operations or operating hours; laying off employees; reducing plant throughput or inventories; closing obsolete, inefficient, or excess facilities; relocating operations to take advantage of lower costs or workers with higher skills; and improving productivity through investment in new machinery, automation, or staff training. For example:

o Several Silicon Valley electronics firms are relocating manufacturing operations to Texas, Colorado, Mexico, and other areas where assembly line workers are available at lower wages. Many of the most labor intensive assembly operations are being moved overseas.

o A growing construction company might decide to contract out operations that were not critical to the management of its growth—payroll, bookkeeping, and similar support services—leaving more time for its managers to focus on bids and project management.

o A retailer with several outlets might close one or more stores and consolidate its inventory in the remaining, most profitable outlets.

Operations Improvement1

The **objective** is to lower costs or improve efficiency by altering the company's basic operating technology or its procedures or both. **Tactics** include automating production lines, plants or functions and installing computer-based control, planning, and forecasting systems. A small business might pursue a modified form of the latter tactic by installing its first structured systems without computerization. For example:

o A large construction company might adopt a computerized project control system to provide work scheduling, procurement requirements, and performance-versus-plan reports. A small construction company might achieve the same results by drawing up task lists and work flow-charts. The elements of project control are essentially the same for both companies, the large company needs the computer because it must handle handle much more information. Other examples:

o A food processor installs a microprocessor-based control system that controls the manufacturing operations by measuring temperatures and other key variables and moving production to the next stage. This system ensures uniform quality, reduces waste, and conserves energy.

o A retail store installs cash registers with scanning equipment that reads the price and the stock number of each item. This allows the store's computer to update inventory on a daily basis.

Quality Adjustment

The **objective** is to support a marketing program—generally, either to upgrade quality in order to build an image of a top-of-the-line product or service, or else to maintain the company's share of the market. **Tactics** include redesigning, the product or service; changing equipment, procedures, or personnel skill levels to achieve the desired level of quality; using different materials for parts or total products; and installing quality assurance and training programs. For example:

o US automakers are attempting to upgrade the quality of product fit and finish in response to competition from Japanese imports.

o Construction companies are paying more attention to details related to energy consumption—by increasing insulation, improving the fit of doors and windows, and so forth.

Distribution Improvement

The **objective** is to increase earnings and effectiveness by providing better or more rapid distribution at lower costs. **Tactics** include limiting the number of distribution outlets, identifying the most efficient transportation options, setting up retail outlets (for manufactured products), and adding downstream manufacturing capacity to ensure a market for raw materials products. For example:

o Some companies create company-owned retail outlets for their manufactured goods; for instance some large publishers create their own retail stores. A more common approach for small businesses is exemplified by a furniture manufacturer who opens a factory outlet store.

o A supermarket chain establishes a single central packaged goods warehouse to receive deliveries from manufacturers, repack items to meet the needs of individual stores, and make deliveries at times when store clerks are available to handle them.

Human Resources Enhancement

The **objective** is to improve the organizational structure, increase worker productivity, and decrease employee dissatisfaction and turnover. **Tactics** include investing in procedures, training, and equipment; improving physical working conditions in plants, stores, and offices; investing in job enrichment programs; establishing innovative work schedules (job sharing, flexible hours); changing managerial structure or systems; and realigning information and control systems.

RETRENCHMENT STRATEGIES

Hesitation

The **objective** is to put off a decision about the company's future for a relatively short time (usually no more than a year) until some specific problem can be solved. A company that chooses this strategy must also identify the reason for choosing it (for example, to wait for interest rates to come down). **Tactics** include postponing investment pending the completion of feasibility studies, changes in the market situation, or other developments; scaling back or stretching out investment; imposing a hiring freeze on all but critical replacements; and scaling back inventory purchasing to minimum replacement levels.

General Cost Cutting

The **objective** is simply to cut costs. General cost cutting differs from other cost cutting strategies because it is usually an emergency measure applied arbitrarily. **Tactics** include selective or across-the-board overhead cost reductions such as salary cuts, travel budget cuts, or postponement of scheduled wage increases; reduction or elimination of certain staff functions; and reduction of inventories to cut carrying costs. The only areas of the company that should be spared from general cost cutting are those which clearly and directly generate revenues that exceed their costs.

FINANCIAL STRATEGIES

Financial Mix Adjustment

The **objective** is to adjust the company's risk--the higher the leverage (debt/equity ratio), the higher the risk. However, increased leverage usually increases the return on equity and the company's ability to grow. **Tactics** include investing more of the owner's personal funds, seeking investments from private venture capitalists, and seeking investments from Small Business Investment Companies (SBICs). Debt or credit may be increased by approaching banks for long- or short-term loans, selling receivables, and taking advantage of available government loan guarantee programs.

External Financing

The **objective** is to increase investment to speed the growth of the business. **Tactics** include reinvesting all or a large part of the company's earnings and securing the maximum debt available, while at the same time mounting a debt structure that will not drain cash flow from other critical areas of the business.

Going Public

This strategy has been extremely succesful for companies with attractive, high-technology products. Other small companies whose products and services do not capture the public's imagination will have much less success with it. Therefore, this strategy is workable only for a limited number of businesses. The **objective** is to raise equity capital beyond what might be available for a privately held company.

Seeking a Buyer

The **objective** is to raise capital for growth beyond the resources of the small business. This strategy may also be pursued by an entrepreneur who no longer wants to run the company. Seeking a buyer may serve the same purpose as going public for those companies for which the latter option is not available. However, if the company needs a quick infusion of capital to finance a new project or product, this strategy would not be appropriate because it takes too long to identify and work out a satisfactory arrangement.

MANAGEMENT TEAM

Key to Success

The management team is the key to success for any business, new or old. Investors and lenders will commit their funds only to a balanced management team. The minimum requirements for such a team are skills in marketing, operation, and finance and experience in doing what is proposed.

In this section of the business plan, list a brief description of key management personnel (include their resumes in the Appendix). Briefly describe their primary duties and their places in the organizational structure. Also list the board of directors, if any.

The organizational structure of a particular company should follow directly from its objectives and resources. Management, then, varies with the organization. You can choose from many theories of management and many organizational models. We suggest a functional organization approach.

Functional Organization

The functional organization approach to management is usually the most common organizational structure. This approach is developed along functional lines (operations) consisting of departments, groups, or individuals that are responsible for such special functions as engineering, purchasing, production and so forth. Depending upon the company's size and scope, all special functions as stated below may not be included in an organizational structure. In this approach, functions are broken down into three categories: process functions, special functions and

Process Functions include:

objective setting

communicating

coordinating

controlling

organizing

staffing

planning

leading

Special Functions are the activities that will be performed by various members of the management team. They include:

Public and political relations

general administration

risk management

distribution

engineering

advertising

purchasing

operations

production

personnel

marketing

finance

exports

sales

legal

taxes

Resources include:

information

technology

equipment

material

capital

labor

land

Management Team - A brief description

Responsibilities

In the special-function approach to management, the management team has two responsibilities:

1. To determine company objectives

2. To organize the company to use available resources efficiently.

In small and medium sized businesses, the management team may be one person. One person can, in fact, perform all the special functions, but this approach is not recommended. One solution is to use part-time specialists or consultants to perform certain functions.

A manager identifies the **Special Functions** required by the company. He or she then *tests* these functions against available human resources as he builds or reinforces the management team. He identifies gaps and develops a plan to fill them.

For example, Tom and Mary Jones are setting up a real estate business. Both have real estate broker's licenses: Mary has twelve years of experience in commercial and industrial sales, and Tom has ten years of experience in residential sales. They might identify the following **Special Functions:**

political and public relations

market intelligence

office management

residential sales

commercial sales

risk vs benefits

advertising

printing

banking

legal

tax

Their next step would be to identify which functions they can do themselves (and about how much of their time they spend doing each function) and which must be or should be done by others. To determine these things, they fill out a chart like the one entitled *FUNCTIONS OF KEY PERSONNEL.*

Functions of Key Personnel						
Special Functions	Tom	Mary	Out- side Coun- sel	Insur ance Agent	Board of Real- tors	Out- side Ac- count ant
Commercial sales		✓				
Residential sales	✓					
Public and political relations	✓	✓			✓	
Advertising	✓				✓	
Market intelligence					✓	
Risk vs. benefits		✓		✓		
Office management	✓	✓		✓		
Legal			✓			
Tax						✓

Next, they evaluate the results. Looking at the chart, for example, Tom and Mary might conclude that the sales and office management are mutually exclusive functions. They might decide to drop office management from their list of responsibilities and hire an office manager to do it.

In short, one must first know what functions have to be covered; second determine how well each function is covered; third, take corrective action when a given function is not covered adequately.

Once management has identified what functions have to be covered, the company should be organized to accommodate company objectives. That is, the organizational structure should be based on these objectives; if arbitrarily imposed. The most common way to organize is along functional lines. A typical example of a functional organization might be a small machine shop:

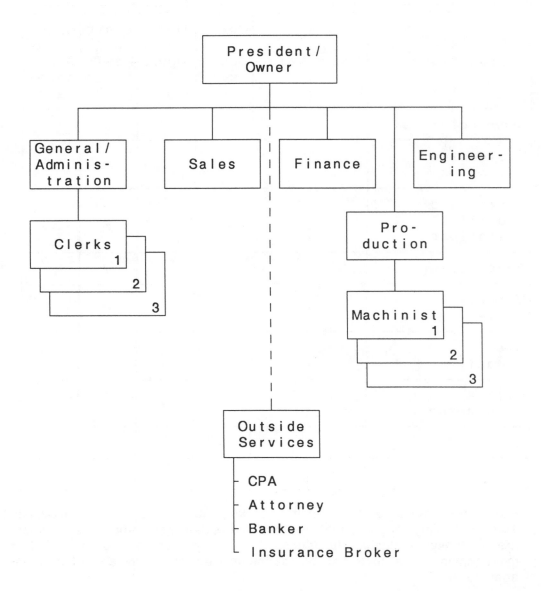

Thus in a small machine shop, finance could be broken down into special functions as follows

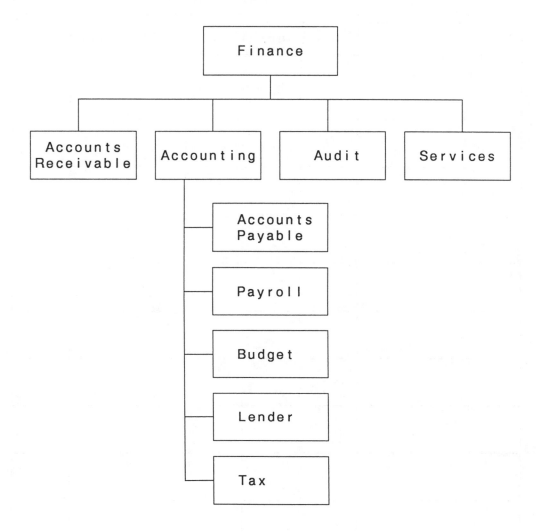

Functions of Key Personnel

The chart entitled *FUNCTIONS OF KEY PERSONNEL* provides another way of identifying the special functions required by your company and also identifies the individuals responsible for each function. Write in the initials of your key personnel at the tops of the columns. Indicate with an X the functions that each individual is responsible for or will be responsible for. If possible, indicate the percentage of his or her time each individual dedicates to each function. Identify any gaps in the management team (and time schedule for each individual.)

Functions of Key Personnel						
Special Functions	**Responsible Individual or Agent**					

Manpower Milestones

Finally, use the special-function approach to estimate your manpower requirements for the next two years. Use the chart entitled *MANPOWER MILESTONES* or create a more detailed one of our own, depending on your needs and on the type of business you are in.

Job Category	Existing 1986	1987	1988
General & Administrative			
General manager	1	1	1
Controller/accountants	1	2	3
Other	1	2	2
Total G & A	3	5	6
Marketing			
Marketing manager		1	1
Sales manager	1	2	2
Regionsl sales managers			2
Field salesmen		3	4
Field servicemen			2
Other		2	2
Total marketing	1	8	13
Research & engineering			
R & D manager	1	1	1
Electronic engineers	1	3	4
Electronic technicians		1	2
Draftsmen	1	2	2
Other		1	1
Total R & E	3	8	10
Manufacturing			
Manufacturing manaager		1	1
Manufacturing engineering	1	1	1
Foremen		1	1
Test Technicians	1	1	3
Direct		6	20
Other		2	2
Total manufacturing	2	12	28
Electronic data processing			
Programmers		1	1
Others			
Total EDP, Per. & Other		1	1
Total manpower	9	34	58

Manpower Milestones

Manpower Milestones			
Job Category	Existing 19___	19___	19___

FINANCIAL ANALYSIS

Financial analysis is an important part of your business plan. Use this section to determine your venture's business potential and its capital needs. You can also use financial analysis to set up a detailed budget plan for your business.

Financial forecasting and regular investigation of financial statements can detect problems that often cause small businesses to fail. For example, the income statement may reveal dwindling sales or high marketing expenses. The balance sheet, which lists assets, liabilities, and equity, may reveal mismanagement in accounts receivable and inventory. The cash flow statement may show problems of cash mismanagement. If you detect these problems early, you can correct them before they become too serious.

The financial statements and forecasts serve other purposes as well. Banks and other lenders require these reports before they will grant you a loan, and they use them to monitor your company's financial position throughout the period of a loan. In addition, annual income tax returns require information that is explicitly itemized in the financial statements.

Pro Forma Income Statement

Complete the *PRO FORMA MONTHLY INCOME STATEMENT* for the complete fiscal year or for the next twelve months. Complete the *PRO FORMA YEARLY INCOME STATEMENT* for the current year and the next four years. Each amount entered on the yearly chart should represent that amount for the entire year, from January 1 through December 31, or for the company's fiscal year. These figures should also be stated as a percentage of net sales. Any assumptions made in estimating the numbers should be footnoted and summarized on a separate page after each appropriate financial statement.

company name
CURRENT INCOME STATEMENT

For _June, 1985_ (month) and year to date ended _June 30_____, 19_85____
($000)

	Current Month		Year to Date	
	Amount	% of Sales	Amount	% of Sales
REVENUE				
Gross Sales	500		2,325	
Less sales returns and allowances	6		25	
Net Sales	494	100	2,300	100
Cost of Sales				
Beginning inventory	210	42.5	200	8.7
Plus purchases (retailer) or	160	32.4	750	32.6
Plus cost of goods manufactured (manufacturer)				
Total Goods Available	370	74.9	950	41.3
Less ending inventory	215	43.5	215	9.3
Total Cost of Goods Sold	155	31.4	735	30.0
Gross Profit (Gross Margin)	339	68.6	1,565	68.0
OPERATING EXPENSES				
Selling				
Salaries and wages	80	16.2	410	17.8
Commissions	25	5.0	115	5.0
Advertising	25	5.1	150	6.5
Depreciation (e.g., on delivery vans)	10	2.0	60	2.6
Others (detail)	5	1.0	30	1.3
Total Selling Expenses	145	29.3	765	33.3
General/Administrative				
Salaries and wages	15	3.0	80	3.5
Employee benefits	20	4.0	110	4.8
Insurance	20	4.0	120	5.2
Depreciation (e.g., on equipment)	10	2.0	60	2.6
Total General/Administrative Expenses	65	13.2	370	16.1
Total Operating Expenses	210	42.4	1,135	49.3
Other Operating Income	0	0.0	0	0.0
Other Revenue and Expenses	0	0.0	0	0.0
Net Income before Taxes	129	26.2	430	18.7
Taxes on income	53	10.7	176	7.7
Net Income after Taxes	76	15.4	254	11.0
Extraordinary Gain or Loss	0	0.0	0	0.0
Income tax on extraordinary gain	0	0.0	0	0.0
NET INCOME (NET PROFIT)	76	15.4	254	11.0

---

company name
CURRENT INCOME STATEMENT

For _____ (month) and year to date ended _____, 19_____
($000)

	Current Month		Year to Date	
	Amount	% of Sales	Amount	% of Sales
REVENUE				
Gross Sales				
Less sales returns and allowances	_____		_____	
Net Sales	_____	100	_____	100
Cost of Sales				
Beginning inventory	_____	_____	_____	_____
Plus purchases (retailer) or	_____	_____	_____	_____
Plus cost of goods manufactured (manufacturer)	_____	_____	_____	_____
Total Goods Available	_____	_____	_____	_____
Less ending inventory	_____	_____	_____	_____
Total Cost of Goods Sold	_____	_____	_____	_____
Gross Profit (Gross Margin)	_____	_____	_____	_____
OPERATING EXPENSES				
Selling				
Salaries and wages	_____	_____	_____	_____
Commissions	_____	_____	_____	_____
Advertising	_____	_____	_____	_____
Depreciation (e.g., on delivery vans)	_____	_____	_____	_____
Others (detail)	_____	_____	_____	_____
Total Selling Expenses	_____	_____	_____	_____
General/Administrative				
Salaries and wages	_____	_____	_____	_____
Employee benefits	_____	_____	_____	_____
Insurance	_____	_____	_____	_____
Depreciation (e.g., on equipment)	_____	_____	_____	_____
Total General/Administrative Expenses	_____	_____	_____	_____
Total Operating Expenses	_____	_____	_____	_____
Other Operating Income	_____	_____	_____	_____
Other Revenue and Expenses	_____	_____	_____	_____
Net Income before Taxes	_____	_____	_____	_____
Taxes on income	_____	_____	_____	_____
Net Income after Taxes	_____	_____	_____	_____
Extraordinary Gain or Loss	_____	_____	_____	_____
Income tax on extraordinary gain	_____	_____	_____	_____
NET INCOME (NET PROFIT)	_____	_____	_____	_____

Company Name
Pro Forma Monthly Income Statement 1986

Item	Jan	Feb	Mar	Apr	May
Revenues	330,000	385,000	495,000	550,000	495,000
Sales allowances	3,300	3,850	4,950	5,500	4,950
Net revenues	326,77	381,150	490,050	544,500	490,050
Cost of goods sold	107,811	125,780	161,717	179,685	161,717
Gross margin	218,889	255,371	328,334	364,814	328,334
Expenses					
Selling (total)	78,355	94,431	110,253	108,355	101,015
Salaries	45,000	45,374	45,750	46,130	46,513
Advertising	12,000	25,000	35,000	30,000	25,000
Other	21,335	24,058	29,503	32,225	29,503
General/Administrative	33,000	33,287	33,575	33,864	34,155
Salaries	10,000	10,083	10,167	10,251	10,336
Employee benefits	1,200	1,210	1,220	1,230	1,240
Professional services	500	550	600	650	700
Rent	8,500	8,500	8,500	8,500	8,500
Insurance	6,000	6,000	6,000	6,000	6,000
Depreciation	1,000	1,050	1,100	1,150	1,200
Amortization	500	550	600	650	700
Office Supplies	2,000	2,017	2,033	2,055	2,067
Interest	1,000	1,008	1,017	1,025	1,034
Utilities	1,500	1,512	1,525	1,538	1,550
Bad debt/doubtful accts	300	302	305	308	310
Other	500	504	508	513	517
TOTAL EXPENSES	111,335	127,718	143,828	142,219	135,170
Net Income before Taxes	107,554	127,653	184,506	222,596	193,164
Provision for taxes	44,097	52,338	75,647	91,264	79,197
Net Income after Taxes	63,457	75,315	108,858	131,332	113,967
Prior period adjustments	0	0	0	0	0
Net Increase/Decrease to Retained Earnings	63,457	75,315	108,858	131,332	113,967

Jun	Jul	Aug	Sep	Oct	Nov	Dec	Total ($000)
440,000	412,500	385,000	330,000	275,000	247,500	385,000	4,730
4,400	4,125	3,850	3,300	2,750	2,475	3,850	47
435,600	408,375	381,150	326,700	272,250	245,025	381,150	4,683
143,748	134,764	125,780	107,811	89,843	80,858	125,780	1,545
291,852	273,611	255,371	218,889	182,408	164,167	255,371	3,137
93,679	92,707	81,738	79,411	67,088	76,129	98,341	1,081
46,899	47,288	47,681	48,076	48,475	48,878	49,283	565
20,000	20,000	10,000	10,000	-0-	10,000	25,000	222
26,780	25,419	24,058	21,335	18,613	17,251	24,058	294
34,446	36,239	36,533	36,828	37,124	37,422	37,721	424
10,422	10,508	10,596	10,684	10,772	10,862	10,952	126
1,251	1,261	1,271	1,282	1,293	1,303	1,314	15
750	800	850	900	950	1,000	1,050	9
8,500	10,000	10,000	10,000	10,000	10,000	10,000	111
6,000	6,000	6,000	6,000	6,000	6,000	6,000	72
1,250	1,300	1,350	1,400	1,450	1,500	1,550	15
750	800	850	900	950	1,000	1,050	9
2,084	2,102	2,119	2,137	2,154	2,172	2,190	25
1,042	1,051	1,060	1,068	1,077	1,086	1,095	13
1,563	1,576	1,589	1,603	1,616	1,629	1,643	19
313	315	318	321	323	326	329	4
521	525	530	534	539	543	548	6
128,125	128,946	118,271	116,239	104,212	113,551	136,061	1,506
163,727	144,666	137,100	102,650	78,195	50,616	119,309	1,632
·67,128	59,313	56,211	42,086	32,060	20,753	48,917	669
96,599	85,353	80,889	60,563	46,135	29,863	70,392	963
0	0	0	0	0	0	0	0
96,599	85,353	80,889	60,563	46,135	29,863	70,392	963

Company Name
Pro Forma Monthly Income Statement 19____
($000)

Item					
Revenues					
Sales allowances					
Net revenues					
Cost of goods sold					
Gross margin					
Expenses					
Selling					
Salaries					
Advertising					
Other					
General/Administrative					
Salaries					
Employee benefits					
Professional services					
Rent					
Insurance					
Depreciation					
Amortization					
Office Supplies					
Interest					
Utilities					
Bad debt/doubtful accts					
Other					
TOTAL EXPENSES					
Net Income before Taxes					
Provision for taxes					
Net Income after Taxes					
Prior period adjustments					
Net Increase/Decrease to Retained Earnings					

Company Name
Pro Forma Yearly Income Statement
Year Ending _____ , 19____

Item	1986		1987	
	$000	%	$000	%
Revenues	4,730		5,392	
Sales allowances	47		54	
Net Revenues	4,683	100.0	5,338	100.0
Cost of goods sold	1,545	33.0	1,738	32.6
Gross Margin	3,137	67.0	3,600	67.4
Expenses				
Selling	1,081	23.1	1,230	23.0
Salaries	565	12.1	636	11.9
Advertising	222	4.7	255	4.8
Other	294	6.3	338	6.3
General/Administrative	424	9.1	466	8.7
Salaries	126	2.7	138	2.6
Employee benefits	15	0.3	17	0.3
Professional services	9	0.2	10	0.2
Rent	111	2.4	119	2.2
Insurance	72	1.5	79	1.5
Depreciation	15	0.3	17	0.3
Amortization	9	0.2	10	0.2
Office supplies	25	0.5	28	0.5
Interest	13	0.4	14	0.3
Utilities	19	0.4	21	0.4
Bad debt/doubtful acct	4	0.1	4	0.1
Other	6	0.1	7	0.1
TOTAL EXPENSES	1,506	32.2	1,695	31.8
Net Income before Taxes	1,632	34.8	1,905	35.7
Provision for Taxes	669	14.3	781	14.6
Net Income after Taxes	963	20.6	1,124	21.1
Prior period adjustment	0	0	0	0
Net Increase (Decrease) to Retained Earnings	963	20.6	1,124	21.1

1988		1989		1990	
$000		$000	%	$000	%
6,147		7,008		7,989	
61		70		80	
6,086	100.0	6,938	100.0	7,909	100.0
1,956	32.1	2,200	31.7	2,475	31.3
4,130	67.9	4,737	68.3	5,434	68.7
1,398	23.0	1,590	22.9	1,808	22.9
716	11.8	805	11.6	906	11.5
294	4.8	338	4.9	388	4.9
389	6.4	447	6.4	514	6.5
511	8.4	562	8.1	617	7.8
152	2.5	167	2.4	184	2.3
19	0.3	21	0.3	24	0.3
10	0.2	11	0.2	11	0.1
128	2.1	138	2.0	148	1.9
87	1.4	96	1.4	105	1.3
19	0.3	22	0.3	25	0.3
12	0.2	13	0.2	15	0.2
30	0.5	33	0.5	37	0.5
16	0.3	18	0.3	20	0.3
24	0.4	27	0.4	30	0.4
5	0.1	6	0.1	7	0.1
8	0.1	10	0.1	11	0.1
1,909	31.4	2,152	31.0	2,425	30.7
2,220	36.5	2,586	37.3	3,008	38.0
910	15.0	1,060	15.3	1,233	15.6
1,310	21.5	1,526	22.0	1,775	22.4
0	0	0	0	0	0
1,310	21.5	1,526	22.0	1,775	22.4

Company Name
Pro Forma Yearly Income Statement
Year Ending _____ , 19____

Item	19____		19____	
	$000	%	$000	%
Revenues				
Sales allowances				
Net Revenues				
Cost of goods sold				
Gross Margin				
Expenses				
Selling				
Salaries				
Advertising				
Other				
General/Administrative				
Salaries				
Employee benefits				
Professional services				
Rent				
Insurance				
Depreciation				
Amortization				
Office supplies				
Interest				
Utilities				
Bad debt/doubtfulacct				
Other				
TOTAL EXPENSES				
Net Income before Taxes				
Provision for Taxes				
Net Income after Taxes				
Prior period adjustment				
Net Increase (Decrease) to Retained Earnings				

19___		19___		19___	
$000		$000	%	$000	%

Pro Forma Balance Sheet Statement

The pro-forma balance sheet statement lists all of your company's assets and liabilities. Use the chart entitled *ACTUAL BALANCE SHEET* for the past complete year. Enter the appropriate figures under the *PRO-FORMA BALANCE SHEET* as forecasted for the next four years. This forecast will show whether your company has the resources it needs to meet its various growth objectives.

Pro Forma Cash Flow Statement

Liquidity, having enough cash on hand to pay all disbursements, is essential if a business is to survive. The *PRO FORMA MONTHLY CASH FLOW STATEMENT* will indicate whether your company will have enough cash for the coming year or whether you will need outside financing. Fill out the line items on a monthly basis. This statement should clearly show how the cash will be utilized. The chart will determine the maximum cash required during the first twelve months and where the maximum need will occur. The *PRO FORMA QUARTERLY CASH FLOW STATEMENT* will indicate the cash requirements past the first twelve months. Fill out this chart on a quarterly basis for the next two years.

Ryck Corp.
Actual Balance Sheet
Year Ending December 31, 1985
($000)

ASSETS		LIABILITIES	
Current Assets		**Current Liabilities**	
Cash	255	Accounts payable	310
Accounts receivable 300		Short-term notes	250
less allowance for		Current portion	
doubtful accounts 5		of long-term notes	250
Net realizable value	295	Interest payable	75
Inventory	240	Taxes payable	170
Temporary investments	100	Accrued payroll	50
Prepaid expenses	225	**Total Current Liabilities**	1,105
Total Current Assets	1,115		
		Long-Term Liabilities	1,850
Long-Term Investments	900		
		Equity	
Fixed Assets		Total owner's equity	
Land	1,100	(proprietorship)	
Buildings 1,400 at			
cost, less accumulated		**or**	
depreciation of 550			
Net book value	850	(Name's) equity	
Equipment 1,850 at		(Name's) equity	
cost, less accumulated		(partnership)	
depreciation of 790		Total Partner's equity	
Net book value	1,060	Shareholder's equity	
Furniture/Fixtures 600 at		(corporation)	
cost, less accumulated		Capital stock	
depreciation of 220		Capital paid-in in	
Net book value	380	excess of par	2,450
		Retained earnings	
Total Net Fixed Assets	3,390	Total shareholder's	
		equity	
Other Assets	-0-	**TOTAL LIABILITIES**	
		AND EQUITY	5,405
TOTAL ASSETS	5,405		

RECONCILEMENT OF EQUITY
As of (current date)
Equity at beginning of
  period _____
Plus: net income (or minus
  net loss) after taxes _____
Plus: additional capital
  contributions (investments
  by owner(s) or stock
  purchases by shareholders) _____
Less: total deductions
  (withdrawals by owner(s) or
  dividends to shareholders) _____
Equity as shown on current
  balance sheet _____

Company Name
Actual Balance Sheet
Year Ending _____
($000)

ASSETS
Current Assets
Cash   _____
Accounts receivable _____
   less allowance for
   doubtful accounts _____
      Net realizable value   _____
Inventory   _____
Temporary investments   _____
Prepaid expenses   _____
   Total Current Assets   _____

Long-Term Investments   _____

Fixed Assets
Land   _____
Buildings _____ at
   cost, less accumulated
   depreciation of_____
   Net book value   _____
Equipment_____ at
   cost, less accumulated
   depreciation of_____
   Net book value   _____
Furniture/Fixtures _____ at
   cost, less accumulated
   depreciation of_____
   Net book value   _____

Total Net Fixed Assets   _____

Other Assets   _____

TOTAL ASSETS   _____

LIABILITIES
Current Liabilities
Accounts payable   _____
Short-term notes   _____
Current portion
   of long-term notes   _____
Interest payable   _____
Taxes payable   _____
Accrued payroll   _____
Total Current Liabilities   _____

Long-Term Liabilities   _____

Equity
Total owner's equity
   (proprietorship)   _____

or

(Name's) equity   _____
(Name's) equity
         (partnership)   _____
   Total Partner's equity   _____
Shareholder's equity
         (corporation)
   Capital stock   _____
Capital paid-in in
      excess of par   _____
Retained earnings   _____
Total shareholder's
      equity   _____
**TOTAL LIABILITIES
   AND EQUITY**   _____

RECONCILEMENT OF EQUITY
As of (current date)
Equity at beginning of
   period   _____
Plus: net income (or minus
   net loss) after taxes   _____
Plus: additional capital
   contributions (investments
   by owner(s) or stock
   purchases by shareholders)_____
Less: total deductions
   (withdrawals by owner(s) or
   dividends to shareholders)_____
Equity as shown on current
   balance sheet   _____

Ryck Corporation
Pro Forma Balance Sheet
19<u>86</u> to 19<u>89</u>
Year Ending *December 31,* 19<u>89</u>
($000)

Item	19<u>86</u>	19<u>87</u>	19<u>88</u>	19<u>89</u>
Current Assets				
Cash	389	438	493	554
Accounts receivable less allowance for doubtful accounts				
Net accounts receivable	381	429	482	543
Notes receivable				
Inventory	264	297	334	376
Prepaid expenses	248	278	313	352
Other	110	124	139	157
Total Current Assets	1,392	1,566	1,762	1,982
Fixed Assets				
Land	1,120	1,361	1,531	1,723
Buildings	935	1,052	1,183	1,331
Equipment	1,584	1,782	2,005	2,255
Total Net Fixed Assets	3,729	4,195	4,720	5,309
Other assets	0	0	0	0
Total Assets	5,121	5,761	6,481	7,291
Current Liabilities				
Accounts payable	341	384	432	486
Notes payable	275	309	348	392
Accrued payroll	55	62	70	78
Taxes payable	187	210	237	266
Other	358	402	452	509
Total Current Liabilities	1,216	1,367	1,538	1,731
Long-term Liabilities	1,665	1,499	2,100	1,890
Equity	3,413	3,364	2,895	4,153
Retained Earnings	(1,172)	(469)	(52)	(482)
Net equity	2,241	2,895	2,843	3,671
Total Liability and Equity	5,121	5,761	6,481	7,291

Company Name
Pro Forma Balance Sheet
19____ to 19____
Year Ending _____, 19____
($000)

Item	19____	19____	19____	19____
Current Assets				
Cash				
Accounts receivable less allowance for doubtful accounts				
Net accounts receivable				
Notes receivable				
Inventory				
Prepaid expenses				
Other				
Total Current Assets				
Fixed Assets				
Land				
Buildings				
Equipment				
Total Net Fixed Assets				
Other assets				
Total Assets				
Current Liabilities				
Accounts payable				
Notes payable				
Accrued payroll				
Taxes payable				
Other				
Total Current Liabilities				
Long-term Liabilities				
Equity				
Retained Earnings				
Net equity				
Total Liability and Equity				

Ryck Company
Pro Forma Monthly Cash Flow Statement 19____
Starting _January_ (month) and ending _December_ , 19_86_

Item	Jan	Feb	Mar	Apr	May
Receipts					
Cash Sales	350,000	330,000	385,000	495,000	550,000
Loans	0	0	0	0	0
Other	0	0	0	0	0
Total Receipts	350,000	330,000	385,000	495,000	550,000
Disbursements					
Direct materials	64,687	75,468	97,030	107,811	97,030
Direct labor	21,562	25,156	32,343	35,937	32,343
Equipment	12,000	12,000	12,000	12,000	12,000
Salaries	55,000	55,457	55,917	56,381	56,849
Rent	8,500	8,500	8,500	8,500	8,500
Insurance	6,000	6,000	6,000	6,000	6,000
Advertising	12,000	25,000	25,000	30,000	25,000
Taxes	0	0	0	167,253	0
Loan Payments	60,000	60,000	60,000	60,000	60,000
Other	49,597	56,015	68,749	75,168	68,954
Total disbursements	289,346	323,595	375,539	559,049	366,676
Total Cash Flow	60,654	6,405	9,461	(64,049)	183,324
Beginning Balance	250,000	310,654	317,059	326,520	262,471
Ending Balance	310,654	317,059	326,520	262,471	445,794

Jun	Jul	Aug	Sep	Oct	Nov	Dec	TOTAL ($000)
495,000	440,000	412,500	385,000	330,000	275,000	247,500	4,695
0	0	0	0	0	0	0	0
0	0	0	0	0	0	0	0
495,000	440,000	412,500	385,000	330,000	275,000	247,500	4,695
86,249	80,858	75,468	64,687	53,906	48,515	75,468	927
28,750	26,953	25,156	21,562	17,969	16,172	25,156	309
12,000	12,000	12,000	12,000	12,000	12,000	12,000	144
57,321	57,796	58,276	58,760	59,248	59,739	60,235	691
8,500	10,000	10,000	10,000	10,000	10,000	10,000	111
6,000	6,000	6,000	6,000	6,000	6,000	6,000	72
20,000	20,000	10,000	10,000	0	10,000	25,000	212
167,253	0	0	167,253	0	0	167,253	669
60,000	60,000	60,000	60,000	60,000	60,000	60,000	720
62,741	59,687	56,633	50,421	44,210	41,157	57,054	690
508,813	333,294	313,532	460,683	263,331	263,583	498,165	4,556
(13,813)	106,706	99,968	(75,683)	66,669	11,417	(250,665	140
445,794	431,981	538,687	637,654	561,972	628,641	640,057	
431,981	538,687	637,654	561,972	628,641	640,057	389,392	

Company Name
Pro Forma Monthly Cash Flow Statement 19____
Starting _____ (month) and ending _____ , 19____
($000)

Item					
Receipts					
Cash Sales					
Loans					
Other					
Total Receipts					
Disbursements					
Direct materials					
Direct labor					
Equipment					
Salaries					
Rent					
Insurance					
Advertising					
Taxes					
Loan Payments					
Other					
Total disbursements					
Total Cash Flow					
Beginning Balance					
Ending Balance					

Ryck Corporation
Pro Forma Quarterly Cash Flow Statement 19_87_
Starting _January_ (month) and ending _December_ , 19_88_
($000)

Item	1987			
	Qtr-1	Qtr-2	Qtr-3	Qtr-4
Receipts				
Cash Sales	1,348	1,672	1,348	1,025
Loans	0	0	0	0
Other	0	0	0	0
Total Receipts	1,348	1,672	1,348	1,025
Disbursements				
Direct materials	249	382	340	223
Direct labor	83	127	113	74
Equipment	40	40	40	40
Salaries	194	194	194	194
Rent	30	30	30	30
Insurance	20	20	20	20
Advertising	64	79	64	49
Taxes	195	195	195	195
Loan Payments	250	250	250	250
Other	191	284	241	156
Total disbursements	1,316	1,601	1,486	1,230
Total Cash Flow	32	70	(138)	(206)
Beginning Balance	389	422	492	354
Ending Balance	422	492	354	148

1988				19___			
Qtr-1	Qtr-2	Qtr-3	Qtr-4				
1,537	1,906	1,537	1,168				
0	0	0	0				
0	0	0	0				
1,537	1,906	1,537	1,168				
271	332	282	214				
90	111	94	71				
50	50	50	50				
217	217	217	217				
32	32	32	32				
23	23	23	23				
73	91	73	56				
228	228	228	228				
275	275	275	275				
193	242	208	160				
1,452	1,600	1,483	1,326				
85	386	54	(158)				
148	233	539	593				
233	539	593	435				

Company Name
Pro Forma Quarterly Cash Flow Statement 19____
Starting _____ (month) and ending _____ , 19____
($000)

Item	19____			
Receipts				
Cash Sales				
Loans				
Other				
Total Receipts				
Disbursements				
Direct materials				
Direct labor				
Equipment				
Salaries				
Rent				
Insurance				
Advertising				
Taxes				
Loan Payments				
Other				
Total disbursements				
Total Cash Flow				
Beginning Balance				
Ending Balance				

19___				19___			

Break-Even Analysis

Break-even analysis is a mathematical technique for analyzing the relationship between profits and fixed and variable costs. Break-even analysis is also a profit-planning tool for calculating the point at which sales will equal total costs. The break-even point is the intersection of the total sales and the total cost lines, thereby determining the units produced to achieve this point. In break-even analysis, linearity is generally assumed. If a firm's costs were all variable, the firm could be profitable from the start and not suffer losses until a given volume had been reached. If the firm is to avoid losses, its sales must cover all costs that vary directly with production and all costs that vary indirectly with production. These indirect costs do not change with production levels. Costs that fall into each of these categories are outlined below:

Fixed costs
General office expenses
Rentals
Depreciation
Interest
Salaries (indirect)
Other

Variable costs
Factory labor (direct)
Materials
Other

The figure entitled *BREAK-EVEN ANALYSIS 1981* is a sample break-even chart. The horizontal axis represents units produced, and the vertical axis represents sales and costs. Thus, for example, fixed costs of $80,000 are represented by a horizontal line; since these are fixed costs, they do not change with the number of units produced. Variable costs (vertical axis) are assumed to be $2.00 per unit. Total costs rise by $2.00 of variable costs for each additional unit produced. Sales price is assumed to be $3.00 per unit. Total sales is pictured as a straight line. The slope (rate of increase) of the total-sales line is steeper than the slope of the total-cost line. This is because the firm is gaining $3.00 of revenue for every $2.00 paid out for the variable costs.

The **break-even point** is the intersection of the total-sales and the total-costs lines. Above that point, the firm begins to make a profit, but below that point, it suffers a loss. The chart indicates a break-even point at a sales and cost level of $240,000 and a quantity level of 80,000 units. If more accuracy is required, the break-even point can be calculated algebraically or by trial and error.

Here are two equations you can use to determine the break-even point:

Break-even point based on dollar sales

$$S_{B/E} = \frac{PC}{1 - \frac{VC}{S}}$$

where:
> FC = Total Fixed Costs
> VC = Total Variable Costs
> S = Total Sales Volume

Break-even point based on quantity

Illustration for 100,000 units:

$$Q_{B/E} = \frac{F}{P - V}$$

where:
> P = Sales Price per Unit
> Q = Quantity Produced and Sold
> F = Fixed Costs
> V = Variable Costs per Unit

Illustration for fixed costs of $80,000:

$$\text{Break even point based on quantity} = \frac{\$80,000}{\$3.00 - \$2.00} = 80,000 \text{ units}$$

The chart shown below further illustrates the relationship between profits and fixed and variable costs. As the chart shows, all other factors being equal, operating profits will increase as volume increases. Note that once the break-even point is reached, each additional unit sold adds pure profit to the company's income for the period. Similarly, a decline in unit volume will result in a corresponding decrease in profits.

Volume changes are not the only factors that affect profitability. For example, by reducing fixed costs, a firm can increase its profit and at the same time reduce its break-even point in terms of units.

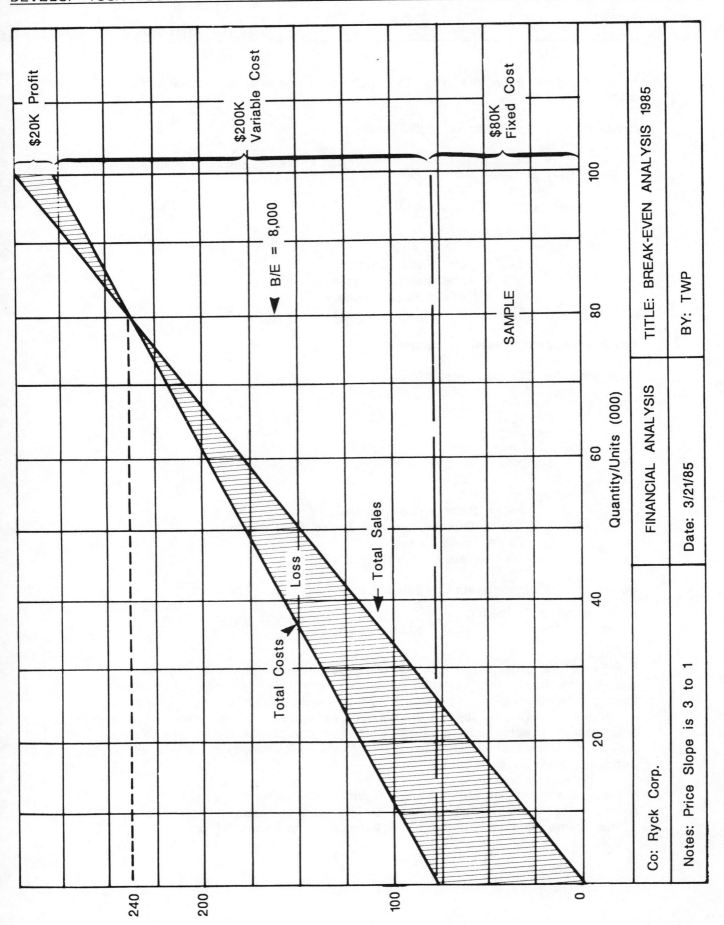

$20K Profit

$200K Variable Cost

$80K Fixed Cost

B/E = 8,000

SAMPLE

Total Sales

Loss

Total Costs

Quantity/Units (000)

Sales

240

200

100

0

20

40

60

80

100

Co: Ryck Corp.	FINANCIAL ANALYSIS	TITLE: BREAK-EVEN ANALYSIS 1985
Notes: Price Slope is 3 to 1	Date: 3/21/85	BY: TWP

Quantity/Units

FINANCIAL ANALYSIS

TITLE: BREAK-EVEN ANALYSIS 19

Co:

Notes:

Date:

BY:

Profits in Relation to Various Sales Volumes			
Volume	Profit	Percent Increase	
		Volume	Profit
80,000	-0-	-	-
100,000	20,000	25%	Infinite
120,000	40,000	20%	100%
140,000	60,000	17%	50%
160,000	80,000	14%	33%

Conclusion

You have now completed your company's business plan. The process, we are confident, has been a learning experience that has produced a meaningful management tool by which your company's progress can be measured and monitored.

The business planning process is not static but rather an on-going one. Many factors will affect your company's performance. These factors include actions by your competitors, general economic conditions, increases or decreases in demand for your product, introduction of new products, new market potentials, and so forth. The plan you have developed should be updated and the strategies and goals reevaluated to more effectively deal with this changing environment.

The business plan is a flexible management tool that will allow you to make changes as business conditions require it. Through the business plan, you now know your company's strengths and weaknesses, resources available, key personnel and their respective areas of responsibility. You also have a working knowledge of the industry, market, and your competition. Use this information to your advantage. The business plan is a lasting working document that will enhance your business growth and viability.

Oasis Press
720 S. Hillview Drive
Milpitas, California 95035

Sample business plan

Now available to users of *Develop Your Business Plan* is a model business plan that the authors have developed to show you how a plan can be worded and presented.

Theis model plan is developed for a computer accessory company. However, it provides helpful ideas for <u>any</u> company seeking outside finances or planning for internal growth.

The plan is presented in a binder with tabs, both of which can be used by you for your company's business plan. (Additional binders and tab sets can also be purchased.) Total price of model plan is only $24.95

Toll-free telephone —
   All states but California — 1-800-228-2275   In California 1-800-221-4089

Name _____

Company _____

Address _____

City _____ State _____ Zip _____

   Send __ copies of *Develop Your Business Plan* model plan ($24.95 each)

   __ additional sets of tabs. $2.95 per set.

   __ additional binders with clear overlay covers (1 inch capacity) at $3.50 each
_____

____ Check enclosed (Oasis Press will pay shipping charges for UPS Ground Service)
   (Please make check payable to Oasis Press.) (Calif. residents add 7% sales tax)
   If you want shipping other than UPS Ground, check which of the following
   you prefer and add the additional charges indicated:
       ___ UPS Next Day Air $12.10 ___ UPS Second Day Air $3.10
       ___ Federal Express $24.85

____ Charge to my VISA __ Mastercard __ American Express __ (shipping added)
   If you want shipping other than UPS Ground, check which of the following
   you prefer and the additional charges will be added as follows:
       ___ UPS Next Day Air—$15.50 ___ UPS Second Day Air—$6.50
       ___ UPS Ground—$3.40·   ___ Federal Express—$28.25

   Card number _____

   Expiration date of card _____

   Name on card (include middle initial or company name if on card)

       _____

   Daytime telephone number (_____) _____-_____

Oasis Press
720 S. Hillview Drive
Milpitas, California 95035

Toll-free telephone –
All states but California – 1-800-228-2275   In California 1-800-221-4089

Name _____

Company _____

Address _____

City _____ State _____ Zip _____

Send __ copies of *Develop Your Business Plan* disk only (no workbook) $39.95

__ copies of *Develop Your Business Plan* disk and workbook $69.95

send disk for ___ Lotus 1-2-3 ___ Symphony ___ JAZZ

__ additional copies of the workbook,
Develop Your Business Plan $33.95 ea   Total $_____

_____

____ Check enclosed (Oasis Press will pay shipping charges for UPS Ground Service)
(Please make check payable to Oasis Press.)
If you want shipping other than UPS Ground, check which of the following
you prefer and add the additional charges indicated:
___ UPS Next Day Air $12.10 ___ UPS Second Day Air $3.10
___ Federal Express $24.85

_____ Charge to my VISA __ Mastercard __ American Express __ (shipping added)
If you want shipping other than UPS Ground, check which of the following
you prefer and the additional charges will be added as follows:
___ UPS Next Day Air–$15.50 ___ UPS Second Day Air–$6.50
___ UPS Ground–$3.40   ___ Federal Express–$28.25

Card number _____

Expiration date of card _____

Name on card (include middle initial or company name if on card)

_____

Daytime telephone number (_____) _____ - _____

Send a copy of the Oasis Press complete catalog to:

Name _____

Company _____

Address _____

City _____ State _____ Zip _____

Add the power of your personal computer to . . .
DEVELOP YOUR BUSINESS PLAN

The sample spreadsheets and analysis forms used in *Develop Your Business Plan*
help you tailor specific ones to your business. The problem of making projections
with a hand calculator is solved when you use these spread sheets and other forms.

You have a choice of formats:

o   Use with Lotus 1-2-3 or Symphony (for IBM PC and compatible computers).

o   Use with JAZZ (for the Apple Macintosh).

The templates provide both the spreadsheets and other forms contained in the
book. They can be modified using the Lotus commands.

Your data is not forced to conform to someone else's model. This model can be
changed using Lotus 1-2-3 commands to add columns, rows or modify formulas.
You can tailor the final output to your business needs.

By using a simple selection process you can create projections for:

o   The Balance Sheet

o   Cash Flow Projections

o   Income Projections

o   Market Size and Penetration

o   Sales Projections

o   Ratios

For computers with a graphics card, the spreadsheets are programmed for graphic
representation. Just use a special macro command in the spreadsheet and see instant
changes to the graphs.

Disks are available for IBM and compatibles using DOS 2.0 or later and Lotus 1-2-3
release 1.A or later (also can be used with *VP Planner or Twin*).

Disk and book (in three ring-binder in workbook format) - $69.95

Disk only ($39.95). *(Please advise if your version of DOS is 1.1)*

Workbook Sections:

Summary Statement
Business Description
Company Analysis
Industry Analysis
Market Analysis
Strategic Planning
Management Team
Financial Analysis

Financial Analysis Includes:

Proforma Income Statement
Proforma Balance Sheet Statement
Proforma Cash Flow Statement
Breakeven Analysis
Balance Sheet
Income Statement

Successful Business Library

Medical Reimbursement Plan, Do-It-Yourself Preparartion Kit
(for corporations with fewer than 20 employees) $39.95

Debt Collection: Successful Strategies for the Small Business
Gini Graham Scott $33.95

The Loan Package
Emmett Ramey and Alex Wong $33.95

Develop Your Business Plan
Richard Leza and Jose Placencia $33.95

A Company Policy and Personnel Workbook
Ardella R. Ramey and Ronald A. Mrozek $33.95

Risk Analysis: How to Reduce Insurance Costs
Gary Robinson $33.95

Managing People
Byron D. Lane $33.95

Publicity and Public Relations Guide for Business
Bruce A. Brough $33.95

Marketing Your Products and Services Successfully
Harriet Stephenson and Dorothy Otterson $33.95

Venture Capital Proposal Package
Wyman N. Bravard and David B. Frigstad. $33.95

Negotiating the Purchase or Sale of a Business
James Comiskey $33.95

Staffing a Small Business: Hiring, Compensating and Evaluating
Robert Worthington and Anita Worthington $33.95

Proposal Development: A Winning Approach
Bud Porter-Roth $33.95

Mail Order Legal Manual
Erwin J. Keup $45.00

Career Builder
W.E. McLeod and Ann Porter-Roth $33.95

Preventing Crime in Small Business
Douglas L. Clark $33.95

Software

For use with **Starting and Operating a Business** series ...
CASHPLAN (IBM PC and compatibles—no other software needed) . . . $39.95

For use with **Develop Your Business Plan**
Disk for Lotus 1-2-3 or Symphony (for IBM PC & compatibles)
JAZZ or Excel (Macintosh) *Please specify which format* $39.95

For use with **Corporation books** (for IBM PC & compatibles—includes
word processing program similar to Wordstar) $39.95

For use with **A Company Policy and Personnel Workbook**
(IBM PC and compatibles—includes a word processing program also). . . $39.95

Wall $treet Raider ... a stock market financial simulation $39.95

Successful Business Library

Oasis Press
720 South Hillview Drive
Milpitas, CA 95035
(408-263-9671)

Starting and Operating a Business in . . . . . .

California	Massachusetts
Colorado	New Jersey
Florida	New York
Georgia	Ohio
Illinois	Oklahoma
Indiana	Pennsylvania
Kansas	Texas
Louisiana	Washington
Connecticut	Alabama
Arizona	Missouri
Virginia	West Virginia
Maryland	Michigan
Tennessee	Arkansas
Wisconsin	Minnesota
Kentucky	South Carolina
Nevada	Utah
Iowa	North Carolina
New Hampshire	Oregon

Authors: Michael D. Jenkins
and co-authors from each of the states
listed. Often the co-authors are associated
with the accounting firm of Arthur Young
and Company.

$29.95 each

Available in 1987 . . . .

Hawaii	New Mexico
	Wyoming

Corporation Startup Package & Minute Books. .

California	Colorado
Texas	Florida

$33.95 each

Title	Price	Qty	Total

Oasis Press

Toll-free order phone

1-800-228-2275

In Calif
1-800-221-4089

Subtotal _____
(Calif. residents 7% Sales Tax) _____
Total _____

__ Check enclosed (postage paid)
__ Charge to __ VISA __ Mastercard __ American Express (shipping added)

Card # _____ Expires _____ / _____ / _____

Name as shown on card _____

Signature _____

(We ship via UPS so please give a street address rather than a P.O. box)

Ship to _____ Title _____

Company _____

Address _____

City _____ State _____ Zip _____